An Ethnographic/Sociolinguistic Approach to Language Proficiency Assessment

Multilingual Matters

MULTILINGUAL MATTERS 8

An Ethnographic/ Sociolinguistic Approach to Language Proficiency Assessment

Edited by
Charlene Rivera

MULTILINGUAL
MATTERS LTD

Multilingual Matters Ltd
Bank House, 8a Hill Road
Clevedon, Avon BS21 7HH
England

The work was developed under a
contract with the United States
Department of Education. However
the content does not necessarily
reflect the position or policy
of that agency and no official
endorsement of these materials
should be inferred.

British Library Cataloguing in Publication Data

An ethnographic/sociolinguistic approach
to language proficiency assessment.
   (Multilingual matters; v. 8)
1. Bilingualism
I. Rivera, Charlene
401   LB1131

ISBN 0-905028-20-1
ISBN 0-905028-19-8 Pbk

Production co-ordination and jacket design by
MM Productions Ltd, 1 Brookside, Hertford, Herts SG13 7LJ

Typeset by Herts Typesetting Services, Hertford.
Printed and bound in Great Britain by Robert Hartnoll Ltd., Bodmin, Cornwall.

To Dick, mom and dad for their loving support.

Contents

Acknowledgements

This volume would not have been possible without the support of the National Institute of Education and InterAmerica Research Associates. It would not have become a reality without the assistance of many dedicated individuals. It is with much gratitude that they are here recognized.

Reynaldo Macias, the former NIE Assistant Director for Reading and Language Studies and Ellen Rosansky, the first NIE ALPBP Project officer who supported the concept of the LPA Symposium and encouraged the formalization of this volume. Dan Ulibari, who later became the NIE ALPBP Project Officer, also provided invaluable encouragement in its finalization. Camen Simich-Dudgeon, the ALPB Research Associate, assisted in the initial conceptualization of the LPA Symposium and through her in depth understanding of the issues which concern bilingual educators and her knowledge of socio linguistics and ethnography contributed greatly to the volume. Mary Cunningham, the LPA Symposium coordinator, who skilfully handled all of the Symposium logistics, helped to locate interested publishers for the volume. The fruits of her efforts are here realized. Eileen Shaw, the technical editor, spent unending hours reviewing and editing manuscripts. She together with Elizabeth Gannon, who verified all references, provided moral support and encouragement throughout the preparation of this volume.

Finally, I would like to thank the National Academy of Education who through a Spencer Foundation Grant have made it possible for me to dedicate time and resources in the final production of this book.

Charlene Rivera
former ALPBP Project Director
Inter America Research Associates.

Preface

The great population shifts occurring throughout the world today are once again focusing attention on language policy in the education of children who do not speak the language of the country in which they are being schooled. The establishment of guest-worker policies in Europe and Australia and politically-motivated migrations of peoples from regions such as Southeast Asia and the Caribbean are some of the events that have brought about this situation. As Kloss observes,

> "Until recently, it was possible to venture an admittedly crude generalization regarding the global issue of language maintenance vs. language shift. Africa and the Americas, so the statement went, were leaning toward language shift in order to reduce the number of tribal tongues, and in the New World, also of immigrant tongues. In Europe and Asia, on the other hand, the psychological climate was held to be more favorable to language retention. This juxtaposition is beginning to get blurred, chiefly because so many American nations are moving toward greater freedom for maintenance — as a concomitant — for the unfolding of nondominant languages." (1977, p. iii)

Although the official language of the Federal government has always been English, historically the United States has not been a strictly monolingual country in either the speech of its people or its governments. State and local polities with high concentrations of people speaking other languages, at various times, have conducted their affairs in languages other than English: Spanish in Puerto Rico, French in some parishes of Louisiana and counties of Maine, German in Pennsylvania and Ohio, and Spanish in the Southwest and New York City.

This volume was prepared as part of the Assessment of Bilingual Persons Project supported in part through the National Institute of Education's contract (N.I.E. 400-79-002) with InterAmerica Research Associates. The opinions of the contributors are their own and do not reflect those of the National Institute of Education.

Current Census data indicate that over 65 languages are spoken by a large number of citizens; recognition of the distinction among the Native American languages would add even more. The linguistic diversity brought on by earlier waves of immigration continues today as new waves of Vietnamese, Cambodians and Iranians enter this country (Kloss, 1977).

The cost and consequences of the different approaches being used in the United States to educate such children are, therefore, of great interest not only within this country, but also to those concerned with the social, economic and political fabric of many other countries.

Schools have used diverse instructional methods for children from families speaking languages other than English. Some have taught in English in a sink or swim fashion or with the variant of adapting the English used to the students' comprehension. Some combine special tutoring in English, English as a Second Language (ESL), with use of English as the language of the classroom. If the student seems more proficient in the native language than in English, some schools provide academic instruction in the student's first language, in addition to ESL instruction. Still others, particularly in the early grades, provide almost all instruction, including reading and writing, in the students' first language, phasing in ESL while the child becomes literate in the native language.

Decisions about instructional approaches are influenced by considerations other than that of the learner's mastery of English. For example, the numbers of language minority students, language diversity, availability of qualified teachers, costs, and attitudes toward language acquisition and maintenance are major considerations. Close to the center of these decisions, however, should be various theories concerning the nature of language proficiency essential for success in school along with an understanding of the impact of the various instructional approaches on the development of language skills and overall student achievement. Often at the core of such a discussion are beliefs about the what and the how of language proficiency assessment.

The purposes of the Assessment of the Language Proficiency of Bilingual Persons (ALPBP) project were, first, to bring together what is known about these issues and, second, to improve understanding of language proficiency assessment in ways that would be practical for classroom teachers. The result, it was hoped, would be to provide constructs for thinking about language proficiency that could lead to practical tools for teachers' use and to better informed entry/exit decisions.

Points of origin

There were several points of origin for the ALPBP project. One was the 1978 Falmouth Conference on Testing, Teaching and Learning (Tyler & White, 1979). This meeting came about as a result of the 1978 conference called by the Department of Health, Education and Welfare (DHEW) to identify reasons for the decline in achievement test scores. Participants at the DHEW conference argued that a significant factor in the decline was the use of inappropriate tests. Using this line of reasoning the Falmouth Conference participants concluded that testing could serve important purposes if it were done in a different manner. They recognized that the use of standardized testing was often inefficient and unreliable, particulary, when used to make educational decisions about individuals and effectiveness of programs. This was found to be particularly true in light of findings from human cognition studies. Thus, the participants urged Federal support of new approaches to testing:

"How are we to pursue this vision of testing merged into a teaching-testing system, fitted to the natural classroom situation, drawing upon the cognitive scientists and teachers and scholars in the subject areas, and exploiting the rapidly developing information-handling technology? One way is to continue and perhaps expand support for research on classroom process and human cognition, and for the development of new technological-based testing, and testing involving persons from the subject area . . . development projects are often excellent sites for fundamental research." (Tyler & White, 1979, p. 2)

Another point of origin was a national survey of language minority students (O'Malley, 1982) and a project to develop entry-exit criteria for bilingual education programs (Southwest, 1980). Despite the usefulness of the results of these projects, their development was marked by some concern for the adequacy of language proficiency assessment measures. The researchers used the best of what was known in order to carry out the *Children's English and Services Study* and to develop criteria for the Student Placement System yet recognized that the time had arrived to put resources into the kind of studies that could contribute to the overall improvement of language proficiency assessment procedures, a view supported by many researchers (e.g. Cazden *et al.*, 1972; Cummins, 1979; Carrasco *et al.*, 1978; Hymes, 1976).

A third point of origin was the enthusiasm shown by many involved in language proficiency assessment for what variously had been called interactive research, collaborative development and developmental research. The notion is that knowledge and application have for too long been separated. More effective research, it has been recognized, can be carried out if researchers and practitioners work together as co-equal members of a team. A few models of such interactive research have been carried out (e.g. Tikunoff *et al.*, 1979; Tikunoff *et al.*, 1980; Philips, 1980; Shalaway & Lamer, 1979) and their results seem promising.

Other points of origin were the thinking that went into research agenda-building for the 1978 Congressionally mandated bilingual education studies, the funding of the Center for Research on Bilingualism, and the bilingual research concerns of the National Institute of Education's Teaching and Learning program. The scores of papers, workshops, analyses, conferences and meetings leading into these activities laid some of the foundations for the project.

The issues which emerged from these activities and experiences precipitated NIE to develop an RFP which called for interactive research and which focused on issues related to language proficiency assessment. The RFP states that,

"Two of the most pressing needs in educating children from minority language backgrounds are (1) to pursue fundamental research on the nature of language proficiency and how it can be measured, and (2) to provide teachers with up-to-date knowledge of language proficiency assessment so they can improve their classroom assessment practices. The purpose of the RFP is to solicit proposals for a program of work with two parts: (1) the administration of a competitive research program to support fundamental research on language proficiency assessment and (2) the operation of an experimental program of teacher training designed to introduce teachers to current research perspectives on language proficiency assessment." (NIE, 1979, p. 5)

Arrivals

How successful has the effort been?

First, educational decisions are not likely to be better than our understanding of language acquisition, language functioning and the nature of language and its uses. While the finest crucible for promoting understanding may be a theory-based, hypothesis-testing strong inference studies, another way of assessing depth of understanding is to determine if it can be applied. In this sense, the project has been successful.

Second, one of the functions of research is to help illuminate the way issues are thought about. It should improve ability to speak in more precise terms, and to refine the debates that go on as people seek their way toward new policies. Although a consensus on what is known about the nature of language proficiency and how it can be measured may not have been reached, the ALPBP project effort should at least clarify points of disagreement, reasons for them, and frame the issues even more constructively. Here also the results were commensurate with the considerable effort invested in the ALPBP project.

Third, there was an effort to form a working definition of communicative competence and language proficiency and to make practical recommendations which would be useful to teachers in the assessment of language minority students for the purpose of making better entry/exit decisions and for the improvement of classroom practice. Here our reach exceeded our grasp and the fundamental research. Although many definitions and descriptions are offered in the papers in this and the accompanying volumes, it was not possible to reach a consensus with regard to a working definition of communicative competence.

Determining how many children in this country are language minority, deciding which of their needs are uniquely language related, and what services may meet those needs are tasks which are likely to engage attention for some time to come. Definitions and their applications may influence estimates of resources needed, distribution of resources, and the nature of programs, as well as the fate of individual students. Hoping for clean-cut guidance on any of these issues is ambitious. They are, however, all important and the ALPBP project seems to have brought together the most that good research, carefully and creatively pursued, can offer at this time.

Lois-ellin Datta
former Associate Director
NIE Program in Teaching
and Learning

References

Carrasco, R. L., Vera, A., & Cazden, C. V. 1978, Aspects of bilingual students' communicative competence in the classroom: A case study. Paper presented at the National Conference on Chicano and Latino Discourse Behavior, Princeton, N.J., April.

Cazden, C., John, V., & Hymes, D. (eds) 1972, *Functions of language in the classroom*. New York: Teachers College Press.

Cummins, J. 1979, Linguistic interdependence and the educational development of bilingual children. *Review of Educational Research*, 49(2), 222–51.

Hymes, D. 1976, Ethnographic measurement. Paper presented at the Symposium on Language Development in a Bilingual Setting, Pamona, CA, March.

Kloss, H. 1977, *The American bilingual tradition*. Rowley, Mass.: Newbury House Publishers.

National Institute of Education, 1979, Assessing the language proficiency of bilingual persons (REP No. NIE-R-79-0012). Washington, D.C., May.

O'Malley, J. M. 1982, *Children's English and services study: Language minority children with limited English proficiency in the United States*. Washington, D.C.: InterAmerica Research Associates, Inc., and the National Clearinghouse for Bilingual Education.

Philips, D. 1980, What do the researcher and the practitioner have to offer each other? *Educational Researcher*, 9(11), 17–20; 24.

Shalaway, L. & Lanier, J. 1979, Teachers collaborate in research. *New England Teacher Corps Exchange*, 2(3), 1–2.

Southwest Regional Laboratory for Educational Research and Development. 1980, *Resources for developing a student placement system for bilingual programs*. Washington, D.C.: U.S. Department of Health, Education and Welfare.

Tikunoff, W. J., Ward, B. A. & Griffin, G. A. 1979, *Interactive research and development on teaching* (Final report). San Francisco, CA: Far West Regional Laboratory.

Tikunoff, W. J., Ward, B. A., & Lazar, C. 1980, Partners: Teachers, researchers, trainer/developers — An interactive approach to teacher education R & D. In D. E. Hall, S. M. Hord & B. Brown (eds), *Exploring issues in teacher education: Questions for future research*. Austin, TX: The Research and Development Center for Teacher Education.

Tyler, R. W. & White, S. J. 1979, *Testing, teaching and learning*. Washington, D.C.: U.S. Department of Health, Education and Welfare.

Background to the language proficiency assessment symposium[1]

This and the accompanying three volumes are composed of selected papers which were presented at the Language Proficiency Assessment Symposium (LPA), held March 14–18, 1981 at the Airlie House Conference Center in Warrenton, Virginia. The Symposium was planned and implemented as a component of the Assessment of Language Proficiency of Bilingual Persons (ALPBP) project. The goals of the ALPBP project, funded by the National Institute of Education (NIE) (1979) and administered by InterAmerica Research Associates, Inc., were:

— to pursue fundamental research on the nature of language proficiency and how it can be measured; and
— to provide teachers with up-to-date knowledge of language proficiency assessment (issues) so they can improve their classroom assessment practices (p. 5).

The LPA Symposium represented a major effort toward integrating both the insights gained from findings emerging from the research component and the implementation of the teacher training programs of the ALPBP project. The Symposium provided a forum where a broad spectrum of researchers, practitioners, and policymakers met to discuss the major issues and research findings which affect language proficiency assessment practices.

Researchers were represented by scholars involved in the development of models of communicative competence, related empirical research, and the development and validation of tests of language proficiency and/or communicative competence. Practitioners included teachers and school administrators engaged in the implementation of programs which require the application of language proficiency assessment strategies. Policymakers were individuals who play an important role in the funding of education research projects related to language proficiency assessment and who are influential in the establishment of policy in this area.

The participants interacted through the presentation of papers, reactions to presentations, and informal discussions. The main goals of the Symposium were selected by the organizers based on the issues identified in a survey of researchers and educators.

The goals were:

— to develop a working definition of communicative proficiency;
— to make recommendations for the assessment of language minority students for the purpose of entry/exit into appropriate educational programs; and
— to make recommendations for further research and to develop a research agenda.

In regard to the first goal, the Symposium participants acknowledged the need to clarify the nature and scope of communicative competence and its relationship to language proficiency. It was evident that some agreement among researchers and practitioners, along with much more conclusive information about the nature of language and how it should be measured, would be necessary to clarify the concepts. However, the recognized knowledge gaps and the diversity of perspectives, theories and research findings concerning the nature of language and its measurement, prevented the LPA Symposium participants from reaching a consensus. Issues which related to this topic are found in the volume, *Communicative Competence Approaches and Language Proficiency Assessment: Research and Application*. The issues addressed range from theoretical questions regarding the construct of communicative proficiency to research relating communicative proficiency to literacy related skills. Language tests and testing methodologies are major topics addressed. Questions are raised as to what tests should be measuring and why. The issue of reliability of currently-used language proficiency assessment instruments was of great concern. Thus, the participants endorsed the development of more appropriate measures.

Issues related to the second goal are addressed in this and the subsequent three volumes. *Ethnographic Sociolinguistic Approaches to Language Proficiency Assessment* has as its focus a multidisciplinary approach to language proficiency assessment and to the development of innovative methods for analyzing patterns of children's language use. The research presented involves what has been called ethnographic/sociolinguistic approaches which places emphasis on the understanding of language use through the observation of children's language in naturally-occurring contexts. These approaches are in contrast to the use of traditional testing and experimental research methodologies.

The relationship between a learner's first and second language development and performance in school are the focus of the volume entitled *Language Proficiency and Academic Achievement*. "A major reason for the confused state of the art of language proficiency in bilingual programs . . . stems from the failure to develop an adequate theoretical framework for relating language proficiency to academic achievement," argues Cummins. He contends that without such a "framework it is impossible either to develop rational entry/exit criteria for bilingual programs or to design testing procedures to assess these criteria". The validity of the framework proposed by Cummins is debated in this volume.

The concerns of practitioners, researchers and policymakers, which relate to the assessment and placement of language minority students in bilingual education programs, are the theme of the volume *Placement Procedures in Bilingual Education: Educational and Policy Issues*. This volume focuses on the legal and practical implications of federal guidelines with regard to language proficiency assessment practices.

In meeting the third goal, the LPA Symposium provided a structure for participants to make practical recommendations directed at influencing federal and state policies regarding language proficiency assessment research and practices. The papers in all four volumes represent the participants' understanding of the various issues. The following is a summary of the conclusions reached and the recommendations made by the three groups represented at the Symposium — researchers, practitioners and policymakers.

The primary concerns of the researchers were:

— The need for basic research into the nature of language that can provide the foundation for clarifying the concept of communicative competence and its relationship to language proficiency;
— The need for applied research that expands on current understanding of the statement of the art of language proficiency assessment;
— The need to undertake validation studies of currently available language proficiency assessment instruments;
— The development of multiple language assessment strategies that include both quantitative and qualitative components;
— The need for adaptable government guidelines that affect language proficiency assessment practices;
— The need for yearly meetings between researchers and practitioners to exchange information and ideas.

The major issues identified by the practitioners were:
— The need for a working definition of communicative competence that clarifies its relationship to language proficiency;
. — The establishment of practical as well as adaptable federal guidelines affecting language proficiency assessment practices;
— The importance of maintaining a network of communication between practitioners and researchers;
— The importance of obtaining up-to-date information on language proficiency assessment practices through more extensive use of resources such as the National Clearinghouse for Bilingual Education (NCBE);
— The use of the LPA Symposium as a model for future meetings among practitioners, researchers and policymakers involved in language proficiency assessment practices that affect minority language students;
— The support of federal agencies in encouraging collaborative research, an example of which would be including as criteria in Requests for Proposals (RFPs) the participation of practitioners at the local level.

The issues of most importance, as seen by the policymakers, were:
— The need to establish federal guidelines that can be adapted to accommodate relevant research findings that have bearing on the application of language proficiency assessment practices;
— The need for federal agencies such as NIE and OBEMLA to continue to support applied research on issues related to language proficiency assessment through grants and other forms of funding;
— The need for federal agencies to support research that is carried out as a joint venture on the part of researchers and practitioners.

It is believed that the work presented in the four volumes will add new insights into the issue of language proficiency assessment. It is also believed that the research and theoretical perspectives offered represent a positive step toward attaining the overall objective of developing effective language proficiency assessment procedures and, ultimately, a more equitable education for language minority students in the United States.

Charlene Rivera
Former ALPBP Project Director
Inter America Research Associates

Notes

1. It should be noted that Multilingual Matters, Ltd. was not the publisher which originally agreed to publish these volumes. They reviewed them late in 1982 only after being introduced to them by Jim Cummins. Although the volumes were delayed in their publication more than anticipated, it has provided the opportunity for the contributors to the volumes to substantially revise and update their papers.

References

National Institute of Education 1979, Assessing the language proficiency of bilingual persons (RFP No. NIE-R-79-0012). Washington, D.C., May.

Introduction

The papers presented in this volume have been drawn together because each presents some aspect of ethnographic research methodology or a theoretical perspective involving an ethnographic approach to language testing that contributes to the improvement of bilingual language proficiency assessment. The motivation for the use of ethnographic methods is a concern with the apparent inadequacies of current methods of language proficiency assessment of language minority students.

While many criticisms have been made of tests of written and spoken language skills that are currently used, the major weakness of such tests, from a sociolinguistic and ethnographic perspective, is that they fail to consider the consequences and implications of functional differentiation in the use of two languages by the bilingual[1] child.

When a child uses one language for some social purposes, and his or her second language for other social purposes, as is commonly the case in bilingual communities, that functional differentiation will be reflected in vocabulary that is specialized in each language. This differentiation will also be encountered in semantic relations, syntactic constructions, and discourse formats that are controlled in one language, but not in the other. Thus, for example, it is common to hear Mexican-American bilingual teachers state that even though Spanish is their stronger language, and perhaps the language in which they have the greatest functional range, it is initially difficult to teach school in Spanish. The reason for this, they contend, is that school talk is precisely the kind of talk that they were always required to produce in English the entire time they themselves had been going through school.

Redlinger's (1978) work on bilingual mothers' speech to children suggests the consequences of such differentiation for children's competence in two languages. The mothers interviewed by Redlinger reported that they used English to praise their children and Spanish to scold them, among other functional differences. It would be logical to assume, then, that a child *praised* in Spanish and *scolded* in English would generally show less English comprehension in the classroom than that same child praised in English and scolded in Spanish.

To carry this same example hypothetically into the testing situation, in scolding, the child who is tested on productive and receptive competence in both Spanish and English would be judged to be Spanish dominant, while the child tested on praising in both Spanish and English would be judged to be English dominant. This is, in fact, what Spanish/English language assessment tests purport to do: measure the same functions for both Spanish and English. The language in which the child is stronger for those functions will be considered the first school-learning language for that child. Meanwhile, there may be a diversity of functions for which the child uses the other language, relevant to school learning, which is not tapped by the test.

It could be argued that existing language proficiency tests measure skills in academically related functions of language. Whether true or not, it is quite possible that the language in which the child has the greatest functional range is the language best suited for acquiring new functions, rather than the language in which the child has school skills. Without a model of language proficiency that assumes the possibility of functional differentiation, issues such as these cannot be addressed.

There is a need, then, to investigate and acquire more knowledge of the relationship between bilingual children's academic performance, and the functional differentiation of their written and spoken language skills in two languages in the classroom, and in the home and the community.

Such information cannot be acquired by the experimental method alone, but perforce must entail the use of other data-gathering methods from the social sciences. It is for this reason, more than any other, that we find researchers drawing on ethnographic methodology to expand their knowledge base in order to improve language proficiency assessment procedures.

Sources of influence

For anthropologists, with whom the ethnographic method is associated, ethnography in its classic sense involves immersing oneself in the culture being studied, living with people in the community for a minimum of a year or two, and eventually occupying a position within the social structure of that community as a participant observer. Some anthropologists view the in-depth involvement in the life of the community (that enables one to explain their view of the world to other Westerners) as the hallmark of the ethnographic method. But for the papers collected here, it is the anthropologists' direct observation of naturally-occurring behavior that distinguishes them from psychologists, who set up artificial interactions and then observe them, and from most sociologists, who ask people questions about how they behave.

It is this feature of research methodology that traditional ethnographers have in common with the new group of so-called microethnog-raphers—sociologists and anthropologists who videotape, film and tape-record face-to-face interactions (e.g. Erickson, 1979; Gumperz & Herasimchuk, 1975; Mehan, 1979; Philips, 1983; Schieffelin, 1979; Watson-Gegeo & Boggs, 1977; Ochs, 1982. The researchers' use of recorded data enables them to describe structure or organization in behavior at a level that was not possible before the mechanical devices that do the recording became available.

The anthropologists involved in microethnography differ from the sociologists in that they are more likely to combine traditional ethnography with microethnography, which may or may not mean some loss of the more traditional in-depth perspective. But both groups have been influenced by Goffman (1962), Garfinkel (1967), and Sacks, Schegloff & Jefferson (1974) in ways that are reflected in common concerns in their work.

The papers in this collection all draw in some way on these two traditions of ethnography. The manner in which each paper reflects these influences will be discussed later.

A second tradition influencing this work is the concern with the relation between Spanish-English bilingualism and the academic success of bilingual children in the classroom. As is the case with the papers in Duran's recent volume *Latino Language and Communicative Behavior*, (1981), this volume edited by Rivera reflects the very welcome emergence of a visible group of sociolinguists concerned with Hispanic populations — researchers who often share the cultural and political concerns of the ethnic minority communities in which they carry out their research.

The plan of the book

The book is divided into two sections that reflect the two dominant needs in assessment that can be served by ethnographic research methods: the need for basic research on bilingual children's language use in community and school, and the need to develop new assessment procedures.

Basic Research

Bennett and Slaughter's chapter, "A Sociolinguistic/Discourse Approach to the Description of the Communicative Competence of Linguistic Minority Children", is concerned with children's discourse competencies as a possible type of skill for examination in assessing a child's language proficiency. They examine the ways in which children build on their own and others' utterances in narratives and interviews with an adult. Thus their substantive concern is one that interests many microethnographers dealing with structure and organization at the level of face-to-face interaction. At the same time, the methodology they use is less ethnographic in nature than that of the other contributors to this volume, in that their data base consists of transcripts of recordings of speech in interactional environments that occur relatively infrequently in the children's day-to-day lives, and have many test-like features.

Rodríguez-Brown and Elías-Olivares' chapter, "Linguistic Repertoires, Communicative Competence and the Hispanic Child", focuses on the use of questions in Spanish and English by children in a third grade classroom. One part of their data base consists of video-taped recordings and transcripts of those recordings, of naturally-occurring interactions in the classroom. This aspect of their research methodology is quite characteristic of the microethnographers of the more sociological persuasion who do not relate such data to a larger base of knowledge acquired through extensive participant observation. Unlike some microethnographers, they have also gathered data on the children's language use in community settings, although that data is not included in this volume. The evidence that they present which demonstrates that children do more questioning, and display a greater functional range in the use of questions, in the language in which they are dominant has potential utility for teachers who express a need for measures of language skills that originate from sources other than school tests.

The third chapter in the section on Basic Research "Intergenerational Variation in Language Use and Structure in a Bilingual Context", Poplack discusses findings of a series of studies of language maintenance and change in a bilingual community in East Harlem, New York. The first set of studies, were conducted to "ascertain whether Spanish was being maintained among the (500–600) adults in the community, what their feelings were regarding maintenance or loss, and whether and how the variety of Spanish they spoke has been affected by close contact with English". Data was collected by "means of long-term participant observation, detailed attitude questionnaires, and quantitative socio-linguistic analyses of selected linguistic features".

It was found that the majority of the adults in the community
— are bilingual to some degree;
— believe "they speak good Spanish";
— do not use English or Spanish exclusively with any domain;
— want their children to speak Spanish as a first language and/or acquire it simultaneously with English;

— feel that "all sectors, school, family, and community, must share in the responsibility of maintaining Spanish"; and
— feel that "most younger Puerto Ricans of the third generation prefer English".

In brief, the data suggests "evidence of a language shift".

In an effort to understand the actual impact of these findings on school age children a second series of interdisciplinary studies focusing on the actual language use of 16 children in the community were undertaken. Poplack found that "the patterns of communication which are acquired early as well as positive attitudes toward learning and use of Spanish combined with the demographic facts ensure the perpetuation of bilingualism in the community".

Poplack's description of the relative use of Spanish and English by the children in community, home and school settings is in itself a form of assessment. She examines children's language skills outside the classroom, in part to determine ultimately how they relate to patterns of usage in the classroom. Data were collected using the same variety of methods, including participant observation, used in the study of adults. In her chapter Poplack addresses the significant issue of differing results obtained through different methods of data collection on the same issue.

This work represents one of the few recent careful studies of bilingual language use conducted in a community setting. It reflects a growing recognition that greater understanding of community use patterns can be extremely helpful in planning bilingual classroom learning programs. It also reflects the increasingly common practice of mixing research methodologies which was formerly not found to any great extent within single research endeavors.

The fourth chapter is by Evelyn Jacob, "Studying Puerto Rican Children's Informal Education at Home". Like Poplack, Jacob focuses her attention on learning outside school. She examines behavior in the home which is thought to be associated with uses of literacy, or learning how to read and write. In her very heavy reliance on observation of naturally-occurring behavior, Jacob's methodology is likely the most ethnographic of those whose work is represented in this volume, particularly in the depth of knowledge acquired of the people observed. Again, as with Poplack, it may be said that the research itself is a form of assessment of children's language proficiency. As Jacob points out, the children's home uses appear to be school uses, or related to school-like activities. Comparative data should reveal interesting cultural variation in home uses, of great value in developing reading and writing programs in schools that build on the competencies acquired at home, rather than assuming the competencies of the white middle-class child. Both Poplack and Jacob represent the growing awareness of the utility of community-derived knowledge about children's language use skills.

New forms of assessment: the Tucson projects

The second part of the book reports on two of three related projects carried out in Tucson, Arizona. All three projects were supported by the ALPBP Project funded by the National Institute of Education, under the direction of Charlene Rivera.

These three projects were a response to the evident need in Tucson for improvement of language proficiency assessment procedures in local bilingual programs. The projects reported on in Part II of this book by Philips, and Simich and Rivera focus on the training of teachers to use ethnographic methods in their assessment of students' relative proficiency in Spanish and English. The approach is based on the premise that language encompasses the child's full range of social uses of language and nonverbal signals and is not limited to just mastery of those abilities necessary for the acquisition of literacy-related skills. Philips describes phase I of the ALPBP teacher training program which was provided in the form of a course on Bilingual Language Proficiency Assessment and offered to Tucson bilingual program personnel in the Spring of 1979. The purpose of the course was to increase teachers' awareness of patterning in the situated language use of their bilingual students, and to encourage them to systematize their ongoing assessment of their students' language skills. Through the training, teachers were introduced to basic anthropological and ethnographic concepts related to language assessment, and were guided in the exploration of the nature of children's language proficiency in both classroom and community contexts.

Simich and Rivera describe the next phase of training which was based on the theoretical and methodological issues introduced by Philips. They discuss a series of workshops held following the course. Through the training, the participants developed an ethnographic/sociolinguistic assessment instrument based on teachers' observations of students' language use in naturally-occurring activities within the school. These descriptions were intended to be used in conjunction with test results in making placement decisions for students into bilingual education programs in the Tucson area. More importantly, through the training process, teachers grew in awareness of the holistic nature of language and as a result began to reflect this new understanding in their classroom organization and management practices.

Both these projects reflect the awareness that teachers do, in fact, play a vital role in the assessment of children's language skills. Both projects attempted to provide the teachers with skills and tools that would help them in their assessment activities. These projects also reflected the need to systematize and institutionalize the contribution the teachers make to assessment. They already have access to kinds of information that cannot be acquired through the formal testing process, and training in ethnographic data collection can increase that access.

The third project, described by Bennett & Slaughter in their chapter in the first section, has as its main concern the development of procedures for gathering information on children's language proficiency. Such procedures focus on children's discourse skills — their ability to develop intelligible turns at talk that are both internally coherent and that build on the utterances of co-interactants in a meaningful way. Their analysis of transcripts of interviews and of elicited narratives with children is in the tradition of the microethnography of conversational analysts, except that they are not looking at naturally-occurring behavior. The focus is on aspects of language proficiency that have not been captured by formal tests, and that cannot be captured by the observation and participant observation in which the teachers were being trained in the first two projects described for this section.

These three projects, then, represent efforts to apply research methods, appropriate for direct observation of naturally-occurring behavior, to the assessment of children's language proficiency in two languages.

The book closes with a commentary by Murielle Saville-Troike that focuses on needs which still must be met in the areas of research and practice addressed by this book.

Conclusion

Some anthropological ethnographers would not view the work presented in this volume as exercises in the use of ethnographic method. There is little evidence in these studies of the in-depth knowledge and feel for a distinct culture that is thought to come from living in the community one studies, even though some of the researchers represented in this volume do in fact live in the communities in which they work.

Many of these studies *do* have in common their reliance on observation of naturally-occurring behavior as a source of data. All also share the structural-functional view of socialization characteristic of anthropology that recognizes the interdependence of institutions, and more particularly, the interdependence of learning in school and learning outside of school. It is important to note here that the qualitative knowledge acquired by traditional ethnographers is much easier to acquire in a rural village of the sort that anthropologists typically live in. As Goffman (1962) pointed out some time ago, however, it is primarily the total institutions of complex urban society (e.g. the military, prisons, insane asylums) that resemble the face-to-face community that anthropologists study in their containment of shared knowledge of all facets of a given individual's behavior.

Ironically, the societies anthropologists study are becoming increasingly complex, so that the ethnographer who remains in the village sees less and less of the lives of the people being studied, and less that is typical or characteristic of the human condition. The ethnographer who leaves the village, and follows her or his subjects of study, such as the Hispanics studied in the research projects reported here, from the village to the city, will find it necessary to grapple with the same methodological mixes that characterize the work represented here. It is with this awareness that the work included here may be recommended to all readers interested in the changing uses of ethnographic methodology.

Susan U. Philips
Department of Anthropology
Tucson, Arizona

Notes

1. The term bilingual is used to refer to anyone who lives in a bilingual environment regardless of how well he or she speaks the non-native language (Zintz, 1975).

References

Duran, R. P. 1981, *Latino Language and communicative behavior.* Norwood, N.J.: Ablex.

Erickson, F. 1979, Talking down: Some cultural sources of miscommunication in inter-racial interviews. In A. Wolfgang (ed.), *Nonverbal behavior.* NY: Academic Press.

Garfinkel, H. 1967, *Studies in ethnomethodology.* Englewood Cliffs, N.J.: Prentice-Hall.

Goffman, E. 1962, *Asylums: Essays on the social situation of mental patients and other inmates.* Chicago: Aldine.

Gumperz, J. J. & Herasimchuk, E. 1975, The conversational analysis of social meaning: A study of classroom interaction. In M. Sanchez and B. Blount (eds), *Sociocultural dimensions of language use*. NY: Academic Press.

Mehan, H. 1979, *Learning lessons: Social organization in the classroom*. Cambridge: Harvard University Press.

Ochs, E. 1982, Talking to children in Western Somoa. *Lge. Soc.*

Philips, S. 1983, *The invisible culture: Communication in classroom and community on the Warm Springs Indian Reservation*. NY: Longman.

Redlinger, W. 1978, Mother's speech to children in bilingual Mexican-American homes. *International Journal of the Sociology of Language*, 17, 73–82.

Sacks, H., Schegloff, E. & Jefferson, G. 1974, A simplest systematics for the organization of turntaking for conversation. *Language*, 50(4), 696–735.

Scheffelin, B. B. 1979, Getting it together: An ethnographic approach to the study of the development of communicative competence. In E. Ochs & B. B. Schiefelin (eds), *Developmental pragmatics*. NY: Academic Press.

Watson-Gegeo, K. A. & Boggs, S. T. 1977, From verbal play to talk story: The role of routines in speech events among Hawaiian children. In S. Ervin-Tripp and C. Mitchell-Kernan (eds), *Child discourse*. NY: Academic Press.

Zintz, Miles V. 1975, *The reading process*: The teacher and the Learner. (2nd ed.), Dubugue, Iowa: Wm. C. Brown Company.

PART I
Basic Research

A sociolinguistic/discourse approach to the description of the communicative competence of linguistic minority children

Adrian Bennett
Centro de Estudios Puertorriquenos
City University of New York

Helen Slaughter
Tucson Unified School District
Tucson, Arizona

The use of the analysis of discourse as a method of assessing language skills has very recently gained a high degree of respectability within the field of language proficiency assessment. The recent upsurge of interest in this area coincides with an increase in efforts to make basic research applicable to specific social problems. For example, there is a great deal the linguist can do in the area of bilingual education to help educational practitioners develop a better understanding of the language-related problems they encounter on a daily basis.

Bilingual education, however, affects a large segment of our society and is, therefore, a highly political issue. Linguists have traditionally focussed on those aspects of language which can be characterized as a closed system. Insofar as language was amenable to such description, issues of social value and power could be considered to be beyond the domain of linguistic science. The socio-political aspect of language can hardly be said to constitute a closed system, since it is subject to change through political action and social interaction. The use of discourse analysis may therefore require more than mechanically applying a new set of techniques to "solve" social problems as defined by nonlinguists.

One of the most immediate contributions linguistics can make in this area involves its highly developed methods of providing detailed and systematic descriptions of the structural patternings of language. There are problems, however, in the use of detailed structural descriptions of naturally-occurring forms of discourse as a means of helping people deal with particular language-related social problems. The first of these concerns time and money. Exhaustive descriptions of given stretches of discourse employing highly refined tools of analysis may not always be practicable in applied settings.

Secondly, there is the problem of relating structural descriptions to interpretations and understandings of the participants in a given setting, or to those who are making use of the forms of discourse being analyzed. A structural description necessarily changes one's understanding of a given discourse by treating it as a completed whole, and by highlighting certain features and playing down others. Alternative structural descriptions are often possible, each with different consequences for the understanding of the nature of the discourse.

Third, there is the problem of making a connection between structural analyses, interpretations, and the uses to which these analyses and interpretations may be put. That is, there are often political issues involved. In the area of language proficiency assessment, the political implications of how language proficiency is to be defined, and of how this definition is to be related to structural and linguistic analyses, are in fact present from the very beginning of the analysis.

The analysis of discourse involves complexities which are qualitatively different from those found in the analysis of lower-level linguistic phenomena. Emil Benveniste (1971) argues that although language is a totality that can be articulated into a series of levels, the transition between these levels is not a continuous one. Whereas the phoneme morpheme, syntagmeme, and so on, are all signs defined by their internal and oppositive relations in a closed system, the sentence according to Benveniste is not itself a sign but rather an indeterminate and unlimited creation. Paul Ricoeur (1981), who has written extensively about the most basic problems in the analysis and interpretation of symbols, texts, and social action, draws on Benveniste (1971) to suggest that the sentence is "no longer the unit of the system of *langue*, but of speech or discourse" (p. 86). Understanding the meaning of a text or piece of social interaction in terms of its implications for the creators, users or interpreters of that discourse, involves, according to Ricoeur, an act of "appropriation" of the world of relations and values projected or "proposed" by the text or discourse. This act of appropriation — whether by the social scientist or the participants — is "the process by which the revelation of new modes of being — or if you prefer Wittgenstein (1958) to Heidegger (1962), new 'forms of life' — *gives* the subject new capacities for knowing himself" (Ricouer, 1981, p. 192). In another passage Ricoeur suggests that "the constitution of the *self* is contemporaneous with the constitution of meaning in the act of interpretation or appropriation" (p. 158).

Ricoeur (1981) is cited because, among contemporary theorists concerned with problems of meaning and interpretation in discourse, he has been perhaps the most acutely aware of the need to avoid a subjective relativism where any interpretation goes, and where the interpreter tries to somehow intuitively identify with the inner psychology of the original creators of a discourse or text. He emphasizes the need for a science of social interaction and of the objective interpretation of texts. Ricoeur also acknowledges the value of systematic structural analysis. Yet his theory implies, as the quotes cited above indicate, a shift of emphasis in the development of a social science of human discourse. This shift would indicate that meanings need not only be relativized to scenes, as Fillmore (1976) has suggested, but that they must be seen as relative to the life situation of the actors.

Discourse as it occurs in everyday settings is open to the socio-political realm, to relations of meaning, value and power. In a recent article Cook-Gumperz & Gumperz (in press) argue that, in order to understand a given piece of social interaction and the discourse produced in it, in terms of its relevance to the lives of social members, it is necessary to see it as 'interactively embedded in the larger sociopolitical context". That is, researchers necessarily formulate their interpretations of naturally-occurring forms of discourse within the framework of a social theory which they themselves may or may not have made explicit.

This chapter consists of a report on a one-year research project which attempted to use discourse analysis to investigate the language proficiencies in Spanish and English of Hispanic children in the Tucson Unified School District. This district is the largest in Arizona, with about 55,600 students, 16,000 (29%) of whom are of Hispanic origin.

Background of the project

Although the research project formally began in October 1980, it had its initial impetus in the previous spring, when the school district formed a committee of approximately 25 district personnel composed of bilingual specialists, administrators and researchers. The committee was charged with developing ways of assessing the language proficiencies of incoming children whose primary or so-called home language was one other than English. This assessment would be used to place children in appropriate bilingual or monolingual English programs. It was expected that the majority of children to be assessed would be of Hispanic origin, and that there would be two or three thousand of these, mostly in the beginning of each school year. The committee included several people who had had previous experience in designing assessment instruments, and who were thoroughly familiar with available published instruments, with which they were largely dissatisfied. They expressed a need to assess more than vocabulary, phonetic accuracy and syntactic knowledge. They wished to go beyond these lower-level linguistic phenomena to assess what they tentatively called rhetoric or rhetorical skills.

Although the immediate concern was meeting demands of the Office of Civil Rights for developing equitable, fair and documentable assessment procedures, many committee members were also concerned that the assessment procedures provide more than a numerical score which, while it could be compared across children, would indicate very little with regard to the particular skills a child might already have. Hopefully assessment data could be used to contribute to the design of better instructional programs as well.

From the very beginning of the project, there were two conflicting concerns. Because of the large number of children that would be assessed, and the limited funds for training and providing salaries for personnel who would be doing the actual assessment, there was considerable pressure to develop procedures which would be quick and efficient. On the other hand, there was considerable sophistication on the part of most of the committee members with regard to their understanding of the complexity of linguistic and communicative competencies, and of the problems of obtaining natural language samples which would reflect these competencies. After considerable discussion and experimentation, the committee decided to use an adult to interview each individual child. The interviewer was to attempt to engage the child in relatively free topic talk first, and then ask the child to construct a narrative based on a short, wordless picture book which told a story about the adventures of a boy and his pet frog. These compromises meant, finally, that the language sampling situation would be somewhat artificial. However, documentation and evaluation would both be aided by having the recordings. In particular, each child's language could be assessed in the context of the interview itself.

The research project

The research project was viewed by the District as a favorable source of information in their ongoing, year-long attempt to refine their elicitation methods and to develop ways of assessing the language date gathered. Before the project had even been proposed, a framework of discourse analysis had been designed which would serve as a guide in initial attempts at comparing children's tapes. This framework became the basis of the research project as well. It constituted a set of hypotheses with regard to the structural properties of the children's discourse that might be most relevant to the assessment of proficiency.

The framework was theoretically grounded in recent work on natural conversation and other forms of discourse. It attempted to encompass clause-level phenomena, inter-clausal relations, text structure and genre forms, and social and interactional phenomena. Major influences on its development were Fillmore's (1979) frame semantics, Halliday & Hasan's (1976) work on cohesion, the general theoretical discussions of Hymes (1972, 1980) and others on genres and on communicative competence, Labov's (1972) analyses of narratives, and Gumperz (1976, 1977, 1981) and Cook-Gumperz's (1977) work on the negotiation of intent in natural conversation.

The concept of language proficiency as seen by the researchers in this project emphasized what Carole Edelsky (no date) in a recent, unpublished paper called PICTURE, that is: "Proficiency In Controlling Texts Used in Real Environments." The proficient child was seen as one able to use a particular set of language skills to participate actively in the learning process, including participating in learning how to expand his or her communicative repertoire. Discourse was viewed, in situations of use, as a phenomenon that unfolded more or less spontaneously from moment to moment, where the creation of meanings, inferences and implications was accomplished interactively between participants. The improvisational nature of the creation of meaning in face-to-face talk, that has been stressed by Fred Erickson (1975) and other students of face-to-face interaction, was the focus of attention in this project.

Essentially, assessment of proficiency is grounded on interpretations of communicative intent. These interpretations are not predetermined and cannot be deduced from the occurrence alone of particular communicative choices, since these choices can typically be used to create a variety of situations, and thereby convey a variety of intents. Participants and/or analysts arrive at interpretations of intent by attending to the complex of themes as they are woven together through given stretches of time. At any given moment in an ongoing discourse, various expectations arise as to what can happen next, thus providing a background for interpreting each next-occurring communicative act. There is, then, room for considerable individual, situational and cultural variation when evaluating a child's proficiency.

However, a method was needed to ensure consistency in the evaluation of the children's discourse as well as some way to document the evaluations. Similarly, researchers needed a way to perform systematic, comparable analyses across grade levels, and across children within grade levels. The framework for analysis was intended to serve that purpose but necessarily provided a rather static view of discourse. The framework portrayed discourse as consisting of certain kinds of linguistic structures, but did not provide a way to interpret communicative intent directly from those structures. Therefore, direct indications of proficiency were not obtained using this framework.

The essential question of the research project was *"What constitutes proficiency in a language?"* Samples of tapes were taken from those being elicited by the District through the 1980–81 school year. The procedure was to listen to a large number of tapes at first at each grade level from Grades K-5, then to select a smaller number of 15–20 for more intensive listening and discussion. During these discussions a smaller sample of about five to ten tapes per grade level was selected for detailed comparative description and analysis. The tapes were transcribed and the framework for analysis was used as a guide for academic descriptions.

There were, in general, two kinds of discourse or genre for each language. The topic talk and narratives were analyzed separately. The framework was not taken as a prescription for what *ought* to be in the discourse samples, but rather as a guide for what might be found. During the course of the year several modifications were made. For example, the use of Fillmore's (1976) Frame Semantics for analysis of clause-level phenomena did not prove especially pertinent, possibly because of the ages of the children. Even the children at the lowest grade level had full command of the grammar of the clause insofar as their use of predicates and noun roles was consistent with the grammar of the language. Similarly, the researchers originally had no way of considering selection of narrative detail, or content, in the storytelling task, and later improvised a modified Propp-style (1968) analysis of the event-structure of the storybooks so that children's selection of narrative detail could be composed.

The richest examples of discourse in the samples used show some degree of what might be called *perspective*. That is, the discourse exhibits relations of foreground and background, or of the explicit and the implicit between parts of a scene created through a narrative, or parts of a topic being constructed interactively, such that the listener can easily interpret what is being said and can make inferences regarding communicative intent. In fact, a good many of the children produced discourse that the adult examiners clearly had some difficulty in interpreting, as shown by their own awkwardness in their interactions with these children.

The matter of creating perspective can be viewed in terms of classical rhetoric, where the concern with persuasion places emphasis on the power of the effective speaker to in a sense create the audience by guiding the inference process through appropriate and effective selection of verbal, prosodic and nonverbal strategies, combining these together without residue. In particular, the effective speaker must engage the ongoing expectations that the listener may have, meeting those that need to be met, adjusting those expectations in ways that allow for something new to be said but which do not lose the attention and understanding of the listener by creating abrupt shifts or non sequiturs which the listener may not be able or willing to follow, since they require adjustments in his or her own repertoire that he or she is unwilling or unable to make.

Methods for analyzing conversational discourse

In analyzing student discourse from the elicitation of conversational topics, the researchers first focused upon the interaction between the adult and child and attempted to reconstruct the interactional and linguistic context of the assessment situation. They determined the degree to which the interactants mutually established and maintained topics of conversation and also noted the degree to which the student elaborated on various topics during the conversation. Samples showing contexts during which rich samples of student conversational discourse were elicited, were compared with samples exemplifying contexts where mutually arrived at topics of conversation were not developed and during which there was little or no student elaboration on topics.

The analysis of conversational data from this study suggested that several different types of "contexts" may result from the interaction of an adult and a student during an oral language interview. These different contexts, *examination*, *interview*, *conversation* and others appear to have a marked influence upon the level and quality of discourse elicited from students, especially that of younger and/or less proficient students. A mutually established conversational context where the adult builds upon the students' discourse tends to produce a more adequate discourse sample. Conversely, an examination sequence, described by Mehan (1979) as a repetitive initiation, response, evaluation (IRE) pattern, tended to result in more sparse discourse production, especially in the younger age ranges, e.g. five to seven years old.

Wells (1981) suggested " . . . a distinction needs to be drawn between talking 'to a topic' and 'talking topically'. Talking to a topic typically occurs in rather formal settings, where there is an agenda or some other means of controlling the topic over successive turns. In casual conversation, on the other hand, the topic tends to shift and change as the discourse develops" (p. 29). This distinction is very important in attempting to elicit adequate language samples from children during a conversational interview. It was found that many children, especially kindergarten students and those at the lower ranges of proficiency, would not talk to a topic; however, most of the children in the sample could speak topically on subjects for which the adult examiner provided some background information and when the child's topic talk was extended by adult on-topic responses. (It seemed particularly difficult for younger students to engage in topic talk to any degree if the adult constantly changed or shifted the topic.)

Older students, i.e. Grades 2 to 5, and the most proficient younger students could "talk to topics" using elaborated discourse when this was elicited by the examiner. Elicitation strategies that were particularly effective in producing elaborated discourse were requests to explain "how to" do or make something and requests to tell about "what happened" in a T.V. show or movie.

Some students, especially older students, elaborated on topics after single or "first" questions, which indicated that an interview pattern would suffice to elicit an adequate discourse sample in these cases. A few students, perhaps perceiving that the purpose of the "game" was for them to talk in an elaborated way, responded with extended discourse to questions that would have been given yes/no answers by other students. In other words, some students needed little in the way of background information from the examiner in order to elaborate upon topics while others gave elaborated responses or even responses of single clauses only after the examiner had interacted conversationally with them over a number of turns on one or several topics. Because of this, the researchers recommend that examiners use questions and other utterances such as comments on the topic, that are *situated* in the ongoing conversational discourse (Cook-Gumperz, 1977), rather than follow a standard pattern of questions in eliciting language from linguistic minority students for assessment purposes.

The importance of the role taken by the adult in eliciting language from students for language proficiency assessment cannot be over-emphasized. Student language proficiency cannot be evaluated without also evaluating evaluator competencies in interacting with students. The adult plays a dominant role in conveying the communicative intentions established during the assessment procedures. Linguistic minority students may not always share perceptions of "desirable" communicative interactions with the examiner, even when they are both from the same ethnic background. For instance, some Hispanic children may assume that standards of respect and politeness call for brief responses to questions while others may assume that more elaboration is expected. It is recommended here that examiners be trained in strategies for providing more explicit cues regarding the social and linguistic context to students who may be unfamiliar with the "educator" expectations of the assessment context and also that they respond to student initiated changes of context.

Since the influence of the examiner upon language samples elicited from students is of fundamental importance to subsequent evaluations, it is suggested that the quality of the examiner's performance be evaluated previous to evaluating a student's language proficiency.

Interactional proficiencies

As the researchers began to analyze interactional and linguistic discourse variables in greater depth, it became apparent that judgments of conversational proficiency in a language are in part judgments of the child's learning of and performance in his or her role as a conversational partner. For instance, the provision of adequate background information and specific pronoun reference, both of which are important to the coherence of an utterance, were often not spontaneously supplied by younger and/or less proficient students. Yet they could supply this information when it was directly elicited. Ervin-Tripp & Mitchell-Kernan (1977) suggest " . . . for a child the 'meaning' of an utterance is not a matter merely of ideational contrasts but an action of social interpretation which has more than a single source of interpretive knowledge as input" (p. 11).

There were a number of interactional proficiencies exhibited by students during the conversation and narrative elicitation that contributed to the development, maintenance and direction of the interactional situation. These included the often unnoticed elements of backchannel feedback to the speaker and prosodic cues that contributed to the meaning of utterances, as well as the more obvious conversational clarification strategies to be detailed below. Particular attention was paid to the conversational context as negotiated between student and adult interlocutor in our analysis rather than simply focusing upon student *responses to* the examiner.

The interactional proficiences briefly mentioned, herein, are those that appeared to contribute to the comprehensibility of the discourse and indicated the student's growing awareness of his/her role as a conversational partner. Interactional proficiencies that were especially important to judgments of proficiency derived from audiotaped discourse were those indicating *an ability to contribute actively to and influence the course of the development of an interactional situation*. The model suggested by this approach to language proficiency assessment is based on the recognition that competencies in face-to-face communication are central to issues of language proficiency assessment. Some students demonstrated an ability to negotiate and/or construct the context of an interaction by:

1. initiating new topics of conversation;
2. successfully shifting or changing the topic of conversation;
3. changing registers or style or reducing/increasing the formality of an interaction; and
4. relating what was said to the knowledge or experiences assumed to be shared with the listener.

Evidence of students' monitoring of the interaction was observed when:

1. examiner misunderstandings were spontaneously detected and corrected;
2. clarifications of the task or evaluations were elicited from the examiner;
3. asides or other comments were introduced into the dialogue;
4. information was qualified or information previously given was self-corrected; and
5. utterances were repaired or edited resulting in improved communication.

Many of these interactional proficiencies are context-bound in that they can be expected to appear only in some conversational contexts and not others. For instance, an important skill is the detection and negotiated repair of misunderstandings occurring during the course of a conversation since such misunderstandings are not uncommon in naturally occurring speech and if undetected tend to break down communication. However, in some conversations, including many in our sample, misunderstandings did not occur and therefore the skill of negotiating a misunderstanding could not be observed. Also if misunderstandings occurred constantly this might be a sign of lack of proficiency. Although it is possible that recurrent misunderstandings might indicate a lack of proficiency, the extensive research in crosscultural miscommunication (e.g. Gumperz, 1976, 1977; Erickson,

1975) has demonstrated that misunderstandings can just as easily be a result of unshared communicative and interpretive strategies. This point needs to be stressed: communication breakdowns do not necessarily indicate a "failure" on the part of the child, as has often been assumed. For example, if a child responds in an apparently odd way to a question, this may be because the child, for good reasons, does not share the examiner's definition of the interactional situation.

It can also be noted that evaluations of proficiency should not depend on the appearance of a particular set of linguistic or interactional features. Each interview and narrative retelling, like all interactions, is to some extent unique. No particular set of features can be predicted to appear in every case, even when participants are known to be fully proficient. For example, some interviews, being more conversation-like, provide opportunities for topic elaborations and smooth topic shifts. Other interviews, being more examination-like, do not provide such opportunities; topic shifts may seem abrupt, while the child does not respond to, or does not elaborate on, topics that are brought up by the examiner. In other words, a particular feature — such as the use of the past tense, or use of topic-shifting devices like "by the way . . ." may not occur. Clearly, however, those children who exhibit a variety of linguistic and interactional skills can be more safely judged proficient.

Student conversational proficiencies: A complex and dynamic combination of interactional, discourse and developmental-acquisitional features

It was found that the task of analyzing samples of children's conversational discourse for purposes of determining language proficiency was complicated by a number of overlapping and inter-related variables, a few of which will be mentioned here. First, the discourse of less proficient or younger students was often uneven in quality, i.e. some segments of their discourse were markedly more coherent than others. This unevenness of performance appeared to be related not only to the context of the elicitation but also to the length of time of the elicitation in that some students who at first appeared only minimally proficient would perform at a more proficient level later in the elicitation. Unevenness of performance may also be related to developmental factors in that some students appeared to be struggling to express complex semantic relations but were in the process of acquiring the ability to use complex syntax and had not yet attained mastery over the structures they were attempting to use. Thus, evaluations about student discourse proficiency need to be grounded in first and second language acquisition research so that expectations are appropriate to the age level of the student. For instance, the acquisitional literature contains numerous references to age level differences in children's judgments about the amount of knowledge shared between themselves and a listener and about how much information should be made explicit. This is one area where differences in cultural background (as well as age level) between the student and examiner may also be a source of miscommunication. Finally, the researchers found themselves continually re-asking the question, "proficient for what purposes and contexts?" when analyzing data. If proficiency in educational settings means that it is possible for the student to talk coherently to a stranger about widely shared phenomenon, then the discourse samples showed a wide range in ability to do this. Thus language proficiency assessment is not merely a matter of determining whether or not a student speaks English or another language but rather how well and to what purposes the student can use language.

The conversational discourse samples in this study included a range from samples containing mainly one or two word elliptical responses, to those containing large segments of mutually established and maintained topic talk, to those containing numerous instances of children's elaborated discourse on topics. Table 1 suggests a relationship found between fluency or quantity of language elicited and discourse variables related to proficiency.

From this table it can be seen that an important distinguishing feature in analyzing elicited discourse is the degree to which the student supplies comprehensible expanded clause level responses so that the examiner can begin to develop a mutual conversation with the child. If, despite skilful elicitation procedures, the child does not produce expanded responses the results of the assessment suggest that the child may have limited proficiency in the language of the elicitation. This conclusion would be more assured if the child had responded with fuller responses to the elicitation in the other language with the same examiner and on the same day. The availability of data in two languages, when there is a marked difference in proficiency between the two, suggests that the student understands the interactional requirements of the assessment context and that differences in performance are attributable to proficiency in the language. However, even here it is well to be cautious about making judgments of lack of proficiency, since there are many other possible reasons why a child might not respond as fully in one language as the other. The child might simply be tired, might decide not to co-operate, or, more importantly, might not share the examiner's definition of situation. Only where it is reasonably certain that examiner and child share the same definition of the interactional situation — including mutual understandings of the goals of the interaction at each point in its progress — can one infer that the non-occurrence of particular behaviors may indicate

TABLE 1 *Discourse variables observable in topic development*

Levels of Elicited Discourse	PROFICIENT: Appropriate/Comprehensible	FUNCTIONAL: Appropriate/Less Readily Comprehended	NOT PROFICIENT: Inappropriate and/or Incomprehensible
I. *Responses* A. Adequate: one word/ clause level	Affirmation/negation Elliptical responses Uses language of the elicitation except appropriate code-switching Answers syntactically and semantically complement questions Prosodic cues given	Ambiguity, e.g. Non-specific pronominal reference Elliptical responses syntactically incomplete/ not matched Answers syntactically/ semantically related but not precisely matched to questions Vocabulary lacking Prosody not effective Gives shut down response but responds to further questioning on the topic	Very long pauses or no response to elicitations Responses semantically inappropriate Responses cannot be clarified by repeated examiner probes Responds to most/all elicitations with "I don't know". Inaudible responses Shuts down topic before it can be developed with "I don't know", "that's all".
B. Expanded: clause level additional information about topic/clarification	Provides information to interlocutor to build topic Provides listener information through clarification	New information partly ambiguous, incoherent Examiner clarification required to develop topic Syntax inappropriate for classroom usage	Topic does not develop (see above) Information so incomplete that topic can not be continued by examiner
II. *Mutual Interactive Topic Development* (Examiner, child — several turns; child uses clause level responses at least some	Over turns, maintains interaction with appropriate responses Provides listener with expanded information	Several utterances incomprehensible/require examiner clarification Several utterances not clarified after examiner	Development of topic over turns incoherent No response/inaudible responses to most elicitations

III. *Extended Discourse on Topics*
Several clauses or more during single turn(s)

topics and changes topics

Adequately supplies requests for clari-fication

Coherent extended development of topic by summarizing or concrete description

Specifies topic through nominalization, adjective clauses, and background clauses (older students);

Relates events in sequential order (younger students)

Shows awareness of the listener by eliciting acknowledgements; checks listener comprehension; elicits clarification about topic selection

Provides orientation clauses, action clauses and conclusion/describes a process from beginning to end (older students)

Explicitly relates one topic to another

Prosodic cues used for highlighting

context from one turn to the next

Misunderstandings undetected

Discourse lacks needed connectors for explicitly showing relations

Background information not provided

Pronominal reference not specific

Vocabulary lacking

language than the elici-tation

Extended discourse not comprehensible

lack of proficiency. However, judgments as to whether participants do in fact share goals and purposes are interpretive and must often be taken as tentative. In every case where a child does not display interactional or narrative skills deemed to be important, further observations of and interactions with the child are needed.

Once a topic has been mutually arrived at between the adult and child, the quality of the child's utterances on a "known" topic ("known" because we can infer this from the child's expanded response) can be examined. In this case, one can assume that the child is familiar with the topic and that difficulties in the language produced may indicate a lack of proficiency. Some kindergarten students responded appropriately to an adult conversational partner on several topics over a number of turns, with the adult directing the course of the conversation, but did not elaborate on topics. This indicated an ability to interact appropriately but these short response-type data were less rich for determining how well the student could make her/himself understood than was a student's extended talk on topics. Many kindergarten students could talk intelligibly on topics, usually focusing on describing action sequences or some salient detail, but omitting explicit mention of reference or background factors.

In making a judgment that a student in Grades 1–5 is proficient in the language being assessed, using conversational interviews as an assessment procedure, we can expect to have data available both at Level II, a co-operative conversation about several topics, and Level III, student elaboration on topics. If the elicitation procedures are adequate and student responses are given only at the level of ellipsis, the assessment procedures should be enlarged to include observations in other contexts. The behaviors described as proficient would more likely be observed in the older students or the more highly proficient younger students. As noted above, it would not be expected that the younger age group specify background information to any great extent but this would be expected of the older students; however, younger students should be able to relate action clauses in sequence. Thus, age and expected language acquisition level must be considered when making distinctions between more proficient and less proficient (or functional) students. More proficient students also grasp the opportunity to engage in extended discourse on topics with less examiner elicitation turns than less proficient children. As related to the classroom context, more proficient students were more assertive in taking the floor and engaging in extended talk to which a teacher would respond. For instance, when asked whether he liked recess, an older child entered into an extended discussion of what he did and did not like about it. A younger student might have simply answered yes or no. Factors such as the student's specificity of topic, provision of background information and explicitness of interclausal relations would then be related to whether or not the teacher understood the point that the student was making and was able to respond to what the student was saying.

Methods for analyzing narrative texts

The narratives found in the samples provided a picture of a prototypically good narrative. This picture reflected the researchers understanding of the expectations of formal schooling and, ultimately, what some people have called "essayist" literacy. In a sense, the most proficient narratives were those which were free of the context of elicitation to a great extent. They allowed a listener to follow the story line without constant reference to the picture book, and made inferences which explained the meaning or point of the events from the perspective of the characters in the story itself.

The following section outlines certain differences in the narrative strategies of the children which seemed most relevant to proficiency differences. The examples are drawn from the English samples but the discussion applies to the Spanish samples as well.

The primary concern here was in comparing different narratives in terms of coherence. A minimally coherent narrative was defined as one which exhibited a consistant temporal sequencing of events and character's actions. Many of the narratives, especially of the younger children, did not in fact exhibit even this much coherence. More complexly, coherent narratives also exhibited relations of cause and effect, event and result, predicted outcome and actual outcome, event and character response, or showed relations between responses or viewpoints of two or more characters.

As expected, there is a variety of strategies available for forthcoming coherent narratives. The data showed greatest variation in five areas. These were:

1. Clause Type as defined by Labov, particularly the distinction of *Orientation and Complicating Action Clauses.*
2. *Verb Structures.*
3. *Interclausal Connectors.*
4. *Prosody.*
5. *Selection of Narrative Detail.*

Each of these will be discussed briefly, characterizing in a broad way the kinds of differences that were found. The importance of the combination of different strategies will then be considered, followed by an examination of their relevance to proficiency assessment. The discussion will conclude with some comments and questions regarding the general nature of proficiency and the role of discourse analysis in helping researchers and educators to understand it.

Because of the nature of the data, the researchers immediately began to encounter problems when attempting to classify clauses according to Labov's (1972) schema. It was found that if strictly syntactic definitions, such as the use of the preterite as essential to the complicating action clause, were relied on the researchers continually found clauses that clearly referenced and sequenced events but did not use the preterite, or even the present tense. Thus while some children used both progressive forms and the preterite in their narratives, it was not always easy to distinguish orientations from complicating actions. For example, in the following narrative from a second grade child, present progressive, present, and preterite verb forms are used; [In this sequence in the wordless books, the boy with his sister, mother and father are shown sitting at a table in a restaurant; the boy's pet frog, which had concealed itself in the boy's pocket, unknown to the boy, is shown leaping through the air toward a small band of musicians nearby] [:The frog ends up inside a saxophone.]

1.   and they're sitting down at a restaurant. Right here there's singing, and there's the frog . . . and the frog, the frog right here, he went inside the thing . . . now he can't sing . . . and then the other man, they're they're thinking, what's in there.

In this example the individual events in each clause do tie together as a single incident. However, it is difficult to be sure how each event interrelates. Is there a reason for using progressive, alternating to a single use of the preterite, following with a present tense, then switching back to the present progressive?

Some children, however, made relatively clear distinctions between orientations and narrative clauses, using progressives and preterites to do so, as in the following example from another second grader:

2.   And then they were playing all right, and then the, and then the frog jumped out, and he went inside the, the thing. And then it went inside, and then the guy couldn't blow in it.

In some instances, progressive forms are used to relate critical events in the story, with alternations by the same child of preterite clauses. Similarly, preterites are sometimes used to describe actions which are, potentially, part of the orientation needed to understand a key event, as in the following example from a kindergarten child [: In this sequence in the story, the frog has jumped into a lady's salad, which she discovers as she begins to eat]:

3. And then the lady, eat it and ate it and ate it, and then, soon, she found a frog in it . . . and then he jumped right out of it.

Note that the repetition of the verb, "the lady eat it, and ate it, and ate it", seems to serve the same function as a past progressive. The same child combines past progressives and repetition of the past participle in another passage using them as orientation for the event in the preterite in the last clause:

4. They were singing a song, and then the frog was dancing. They got louder and louder and louder. And then the man was looking inside the horn, he didn't know what it was, and they all got angry, and then the frog jumped on the man's head.

In general, for the older children, the clearer was the distinction between orientation and action clauses and the easier it became to apply syntactic criteria to the classification of clauses.

A variety of verb structures was found in the narratives, including present and past progressives, preterites, BE plus Going plus Infinitive (as in *was going to jump*) and past perfects. In many narratives, character responses to events are put in the progressive form. This gives the responses the appearance of being detached from the event from the point of view of the person constructing the text, as in the following third grade narrative:

5. The frog fell on the man's face, and he falls and breaks the drum, and they're laughing, and he's angry, and he's angry, and they're laughing.

There is a variety of interclausal connectors to be found in the narratives. However, the most common ones are *and* and *and then*, which allow only for a simple sequencing of events. Some children showed the ability to use subordinating conjunctions in order to place one part of an event in the background for another, as in the following example from a fourth grader:

6. When the man went to drink his wine, the frog kissed him.

On the other hand, some of the narratives use almost no interclausal connectors, as in the following 5th grade example:

7.   The man's gonna catch the frog. Those other people are leaving. He catches it.

As regards prosody, there are two aspects where variation seemed important. One involved the use of what might be called prosodic genre marking. That is, some children used a prosodic style that was recognizable as an oral reading style, thus defining the task as an oral reading, where the listener's role is to remain silent throughout. Others used a repeated low-rising tone at the end of each utterance, as in the last example, which helped to define the task as something more like a test, with the listener put in the examiner role. Many examiners, when confronted with this pattern, in fact often provided backchannel feedback after clauses with this rising pattern. Similarly, some children used prosodic modulations to mimic speech patterns in quoted speech of characters, although this was relatively rare. Usually dialogue was marked in this way only when an oral reading style was also used, as in the following excerpt from a 5th grader:

8.   The waiter said, "What would you order?" Then, they all looked at the menu. Petey said, "I'll order hamburger and french fries". The dad said, 'I'll order a big steak". The little girl said, "I'll order . . . fish". The band kept on playing. Something was the matter with this man's saxophone. "Whatsa matter with this thing!"

The other aspect of prosody that was of interest concerned its use, or lack of use, to mark relationships of meaning across clauses. In an example given earlier, a fourth grade child uses a rising-falling tone at the end of a *when* clause, to cue the listener that the main bit of information is about to come. She places high stress on the action verb in the following clause:

6.   When the man went to drink his wine, the frog kissed him.

However, many children used very minimal prosodic modulations, or none at all to signal relationships of information of this kind. In another example cited earlier, a fifth grade child uses only low-rises at the end of each clause. Since the clauses also have no connectors, relationships of foreground and background are not very well established, so that the listener cannot predict as easily how each new clause is to be related to prior ones:

7.   The man's gonna catch the frog. Those other people are leaving. He catches it.

Finally there was considerable variation in selection of narrative detail. Our modified Proppian analysis showed that the frog books exhibited a three-part structure bracketed by an introductory section at the beginning, and a coda or resolution at the end. The three-part structure involved three episodes in which the frog violated a convention, rule or interdiction, resulting in disruption of the normal state of affairs, and in characters responding to the disruption in various ways. The youngest children seldom kept distinct the introductory part of the story from the initial episode of violation. Also, they often neglected to mention the violation in an episode, even if they had prepared the listener by referencing the conditions that led up to the violation. Again, younger children did not always explicitly relate character responses to the violations. The result was often a sort of hodge-podge which was minimally coherent, if at all, as in the following second grade example: [in this episode the frog accidentally lands in a man's wineglass as he holds it up and to the side, as if offering a toast; when he goes to drink, the frog kisses him on the nose]:

10. And then he went inside the cup, this is a cup, and then he was sad, and she was mad, and he was mad, then he came out, and then he got mad, he wanted to drink it.

It is interesting, in this last example, that the character's responses are given, but the event to which they are responding is not in fact mentioned.

It should be stated at this point that, while it is a relatively simple matter to compare narratives under each of the above categories, it is somewhat more difficult to relate these directly to judgments of narrative coherence. This is because, as the discussion of prosody above may have indicated, strategies on different levels can be combined, or a strategy on one level may be used to serve functions other strategies can also serve, as in the use of prosody to mark relations of information between clauses, even when explicit clausal connectors are *not* used. Simply totalling up the numbers and kinds of strategies children used did not provide a characterization of coherence that in every case corresponded with the researchers' intuitive judgments of coherence upon hearing the tape, or reading the transcripts. Each sample had therefore to be examined in the light of the researchers' interpretations. If it was agreed that a particular passage lacked coherence, it was then examined in order to see what kinds of cues might have been used that were missing. However, these intuitive judgments were themselves necessarily based on the researchers' own expectations of what a coherent narrative would be like, and of course these expectations were governed by their own social and cultural background, and were no doubt particularly influenced by their training in literacy. This is not to say that these judgments were either valid or invalid, but only to point out that they were necessarily relative.

Finally, to conclude with some questions regarding the general nature of language proficiency, the problems of assessing it, and the role of discourse analysis in helping to understand it, it should be pointed out first that the performance of each child had to be seen as relative to the situation of elicitation. Thus, a child who uses a somewhat montonous rising tone at the end of each clause, as in one of the examples given earlier, is not necessarily incapable of other kinds of prosodic modulation in a task of this kind, but may well be interpreting the task as a test of his or her ability to identify and describe what he or she sees in each picture as the page is turned. The general guideline used in this study was that if a child did not display a particular skill, he or she could not necessarily be said not to have the use of that skill. The District is not, in fact, attempting to use the discourse elicitations as the only source of their judgments of a child's proficiency. Children who do not appear proficient are then observed in the classroom by teachers who have been trained in the rudiments of ethnographic observation, and who are familiar with the criteria used to assess the discourse samples.

More difficult is the question of defining proficiency. If one attempts to provide a practical answer, such as the one the researchers began their project with, a problem arises. Their original concern was with determining whether the child could function in a classroom in which a particular language was being used. However, ethnographic studies, particularly cross-cultural studies, have shown that what is acceptable or appropriate communicative behavior in one classroom is not necessarily so in another.

The question of whether a child is proficient in a language, and of what constitutes proficiency in general, cannot be separated from other questions which are less strictly linguistic in nature, such as, "Proficiency for what purposes?". The researchers' working judgements of narrative coherence were based on their own background in the uses and forms of essayist literacy. However, anthropologists who have studied narratives cross-culturally, such as Ron and Suzanne Scollon, (1981) and A. L. Becker (1979) have shown that narrative coherence and structure is not necessarily a universal, non-malleable feature of all narratives. Rather, it varies culturally and situationally within a given culture.

The scope of this project was limited to comparative descriptions of artificially elicited samples of discourse. This kind of research needs to be supplemented by ethnographic observation, not only of the forms and uses of discourse in the classroom and school playground, but in other community environments as well. However, simply gathering more data on forms of discourse in other settings is itself not sufficient to answer the question of what constitutes proficiency in a language. Rather, this sort of investigation needs to be framed in a larger investigation of the uses these forms are, or can be, put to. Such an analysis cannot simply be cognitive in nature, nor can it succeed if it views communication merely as the transmission of information. As Michal Foucault (1980) has pointed out, the forms of discourse by means of which we make sense of our lives are themselves political in nature, even where they appear most neutral. The question of language proficiency needs to be cast in the light of an examination of the element of power in discourse; as Foucault puts it,

"In any society, there are manifold relations of power which permeate, characterize, and constitute the social body, and these relations of power cannot themselves be established, consolidated nor implemented without the production, accumulation, circulation, and functioning of a discourse. Posing for discourse the question of power means basically to ask whom does discourse serve?" (p. 93)

Although the two topics of examining children's discourse skills and questions of political power may seem to be unrelated, it can be suggested here that, in fact, the question of what proficiencies are parcelled out to what social groups in our society, and to what ends, is *the* essential question of language proficiency.

Conclusion

Finally, it is necessary to re-emphasize three important themes which have been touched upon briefly. First, it needs to be stressed that when a child does not produce much language in an elicitation — no matter how much care is given to creating a "natural" context — judgments of proficiency cannot be reliably based on that elicitation alone. There can be many reasons, some of them nonlinguistic, for *not* producing speech. It might be noted here that the elicitation sessions from which the data were drawn have a built-in oddness, in that first a child is asked to speak solely in one language (Spanish), then solely in another (English). The switch from Spanish to English is determined by the examiner, or rather by the design of the elicitation itself. Once the interview and narrative in Spanish are completed, the examiner must switch to English. The transition might, of course, be made in a gradual way, though, in having the child do nearly identical tasks in the two languages, it is difficult not to create the aura of a testing situation. Children, especially those in the intermediate or higher grades, are likely to sense they are there to be evaluated, a situation that may have built-in negative connotations for some of them. In this connection, it is important to recognize that a child who produces minimal responses, such as short, elliptical answers to questions, may be skilfully employing a strategy of minimal co-operation. That is, "lack" of language production, far from indicating an inability, may sometimes correlate with proficiency. At the same time, it is clear that a child who produces little language in the elicitation should be observed and interacted with in a variety of other settings in order to provide a more reliable basis for evaluation.

Secondly, the complexity, flexibility and range of linguistic and interactional skills that even very young children have command of are quite vast, as recent work on children's conversational and discourse skills has begun to demonstrate (Ervin-Tripp & Mitchell-Kernan, 1977). It is unlikely that any single test can be designed which will reliably sample an adequate range of a proficient child's skills. Thus even where a child does exhibit a variety of proficiencies in an elicitation, there is no reason to assume this exhausts that child's abilities. For the purposes of program placement, of course, it may not be immediately necessary to sample such a child's language skills in other settings, nor may it be practicable, given the constraints of time, money and personnel school districts usually operate with.

This latter point brings us to a third theme. In the first two themes, limitations of elicitations for evaluating language proficiency were emphasized. Here the stress is on the value of getting recorded samples of speech as produced in interactional settings, even where these settings are admittedly artificial to some extent. For one thing, examiners skilled enough in interacting with children can allow the interaction to be flexible and to "go with" the flow of the interaction as partly determined by the child. Examiners can actively encourage the child's participation by listening to and responding to what the child says and does, rather than having to focus their attention on testing particular performance abilities. Opportunities for the display of conversational skills that are used in other situations can be provided for that other, more highly structured tests aimed at testing specific competencies (such as the *Bilingual Syntax Measure* [Burt *et al*, 1975]), may miss. That is, if one's goal, as examiner, is to find out whether a child has command of negation, one is likely to see a very different child — linguistically speaking — than if one's goal is to establish a conversational interaction with the child.

Although there are implications that need to be stressed, they cannot be elaborated on here. By getting samples of discourse, whether through elicitation, observation or simply through casual interaction, one begins to get a picture both of what children can do and what they actually do. Such samples can only be evaluated in terms of participants' mutual definition of the ongoing situation: judgments of proficiency are based on judgments of communicative intent. But no interactional context is isolated from the institutions and socio-political contexts which "surround" it, as it were. By focusing attention on the relations between contexts, meanings, intentions, linguistic and discourse strategies, and judgments of proficiency, a sociolinguistic/discourse approach to language proficiency assessment could form the beginnings of a more general critique of the way of language use and their associated ways of life we want to teach, actually teach, or fail to teach.

References

Becker, A. L. 1979, Text-building, epistomology, and aesthetics in Japanese shadow theatre. In A. L. Becker & A. A. Yengoyon (eds), *The imagination of reality: Essays in Southeast Asia coherent systems*. Norwood, N. J.: Ablex Publishing Co.

Burt, M. K., Dulay, H. & Hernandez Chavez, E. 1975, *Bilingual Syntax Measure*. New York: Psychological Corporation.

Benveniste, E. 1971, *Problems in general linguistics*. Miami, FA: University of Florida Press.

Cook-Gumperz, J. 1977, Situated instructions: Language sociologation of school age children. In S. Ervin-Tripp & O. Mitchell-Kernan (eds), *Child discourse*. New York: Academic Press.

Cook-Gumperz, J. & Gumperz, J. J. in press, From oral to written culture: The transition to literacy. In M. F. Whitehead (ed.), *Variation in writing*. New York: Erlbaum Associates.

Edelsky, C. Proficiency in controlling texts used in real environment (PICTURE). *A language deficit theory for the Eighties: CALP, BICS and semi-lingualism*. Unpublished manuscript, Arizona State Elementary Education Department.

Erickson, F. 1975, *Gatekeeping and the melting pot: Interaction in counseling interview*. Harvard Educational Review, 45(1), 44–70.

Ervin-Tripp, S., & Mitchell-Kernan, C. 1977, *Child discourse*. New York: Academic Press

Fillmore, C. J. 1976, The need for a frame semantics in linguistics. In *Statistical methods in linguistics*. Stockholm: Skriptor.

— 1979, On Fluency. In C. J. Fillmore, W. S-Y Wang & D. Kempler (eds), *Individual differences in language ability and language behavior*. New York: Academic Press

Foucault, M. 1980, *Power/Knowledge*. New York: Panthern Books

Gumperz, J. J. 1976, Language communication and public negotiation. In P. Sanday (ed.), *Anthropology and the public interest: Fieldwork and theory*. New York: Academic Press.

— 1977, Sociocultural knowledge in conversational inference. In M. Saville-Troike (ed.), *Twenty-eighth Annual Round Table Series on Language and Linguistics*. Washington, D.C.: Georgetown University Press.

— 1981, Conversational inference and classroom learning. In J. Green & C. Wallat (eds), *Ethnography and language in educational settings*. Norwood, NJ: Ablex Publishing Corp.

Halliday, M. A. K. & Hasan, R. 1976, *Cohesion in English*, London: Longman Group.

Heidegger, M. 1962, *Being and time*. New York: Harper & Row.

Hymes, D. 1972, *Introduction to functions of language in the classroom*. New York: Teachers College Press.

— 1980, *Language in education: Ethnolinguistic essays*. Washington, D.C.: Center for Applied Linguistics.

Labov, W. 1972, *Language in the inner city*. Philadelphia: University of Pennsylvania Press.

Meham, H. 1979, *Learning lessons: Social organization in the classroom*. Cambridge, Mass.: Harvard University Press

Propp, V. 1968, *Morphology of the folktale*. Austin, TX: University of Texas Press.

Ricoeur, P. 1981, *Hemeneutics and the human sciences*. London: Cambridge University Press.

Scollon, R. & Scollon S. 1981, *Narrative, literacy and face in interethnic communication*. Norwood, NJ: Ablex Publishing Co.

Wells, G., *et al.* 1981, *Learning through interaction: The study of language development*. New York: Cambridge University Press.

Wittgenstein, L. 1958, *Philosophical investigations*. New York: Macmillan.

Linguistic repertoires, communicative competence and the hispanic child

Flora Rodríguez-Brown and Lucia Elías-Olivares
University of Illinois, Chicago

Studies dealing with the languages used by bilingual children have generally focused on the individual speaker's capacity to form and comprehend sentences in the standard variety of one of the two languages (González, 1970; Lance, 1975). Language behavior in specific speech situations within a speech community has been the concern of more recent studies which have examined bilingual speech (Poplack, 1979; Zentella, 1978; McClure, 1977). These studies have taken as a starting point the speech community as a whole and have examined the structure of the total range of styles available to the speakers through the use of sociolinguistic and ethnographic methodologies. Speech community, speech event, speech act, verbal repertoire and communicative competence have been the basic concepts used in such research because they are fundamental to understanding how language is used in different settings (Blom & Gumperz, 1972; Gumperz, 1964; Hymes, 1974). Several studies have demonstrated that there are no single style speakers and that most speakers move along a continuum of linguistic varieties whose selection depends on sociolinguistic factors such as types of speech events, attitudes toward varieties, formality or informality of the speech situation, age, sex, education, etc. (Hernández-Chávez, 1978; Labov, 1966; Peñalosa, 1979). The languages and linguistic varieties — dialects, languages, styles, and registers — available to members of a speech community in the home, the neighborhood and the school constitute their linguistic or verbal repertoire.

If one agrees that speech is primarily social behavior, and that it should not be limited to the production of grammatically correct sentences, then one can argue as Hymes does that:

"A child from whom any and all of the grammatical sentences of a language might come with equal likelihood would be of course a social monster. Within the social matrix in which it acquires a system of grammar, a child acquires also a system of its use, regarding persons, places, purposes, other models of communication, etc. — all the components of communicative events, together with attitudes and beliefs regarding them. There also develop patterns of the sequential use of language in conversation, address, standard routines, and the like. In such acquisition resides the child's sociolinguistic competence (or, more broadly, communicative competence), its ability to participate in its society as not only a speaking, but also a communicating member. What children so acquire, an integrated theory of sociolinguistic description must be able to describe." (Hymes, 1974, p. 75)

From this perspective, the basic unit for the analysis of the interaction of language and social setting is the communicative event (Hymes, 1974).

Some researchers have not only examined language behavior in specific speech situations, but have also changed the unit of analysis from the sentence to speech acts and events. Current research dealing with discourse structure focuses on turns of speaking, conversations, moves, utterances, and exchanges (Ervin-Tripp & Mitchell-Kernan, 1977; Sinclair & Coulthard, 1975). This research has focused on diversity in language where it has been found that there is not always a direct correspondence between linguistic functions and structural forms. Questions, for example, are difficult to code because some questions can be interpreted as requests for information, others as imbedded imperatives, while still others as simply rhetorical (Ervin-Tripp, 1977). Thus, the function of an interrogative, declarative or imperative sentence may be served by different forms. Because any given speech act can include several grammatical structures, and any given grammatical structure can be used to perform several communicative acts, there may, sometimes, be a lack of correspondence between form and function (Coulthard, 1977; Hymes, 1971).

Dore (1977) indicates that form alone cannot determine pragmatic function because the hearer's interpretation of the speaker's communicative intent is dependent on various factors that function independently of the grammar. The first step in the formalization of the analysis of the functional use of speech according to Labov is to distinguish "what is being said from what is being done" (Labov, 1972, p. 121). This type of analysis must relate a smaller number of sentences written within a grammatical framework to a much larger set of actions accomplished with words.

With bilingual children, the specification of the context in which each or both languages are used is relevant because to say that children are dominant or more proficient in English or Spanish is insufficient. Shuy points out that in order to begin to assess language abilities accurately, one must assess comparative language abilities in a broad number of contexts, specifying in detail where, under what circumstances, and to what extent each language is used, as well as the relationships among those contexts (Shuy, 1977). Thus, in order to answer the question whether a child is more dominant or more proficient in English at school, in the neighbourhood playground, or with her or his siblings, one must consider not only a quantitative dimension but a qualitative dimension as well, e.g. conversations with peers and siblings or formal interactions with teachers, and performance within various speech functions such as requesting and giving information, commanding, persuading or complaining (Hernández-Chávez, 1978). In short, a holistic approach examines language use in specific situations, with different interlocutors and for different purposes.

Traditionally, testing situations which are monolingually defined tend to reduce the speaker's linguistic repertoire. Lavandera (1978) points out that it is only in bilingually defined settings and situations that the bilingual's total verbal repertoire is used. That is, the speaker is able to activate all the varieties possessed by him or her, mix them (code-switch), and thus take advantage of his or her range of communicative competence.

The study, which is described in this paper, focused on the assessment of communicative competence of children who are at different levels of proficiency in English and Spanish. The approach used was a sociolinguistic/ethnographic one. The purpose of the study was to examine the extent to which children use questions at different levels of proficiency in Spanish and English. Several of the components of the communicative events were used for the study. They are: (1) the various kinds of participants and their sociological attributes; (2) the mode of communication: either verbal or written; (3) the linguistic varieties shared by the participants; (4) the setting: home, neighborhood, classroom; (5) the intent or purpose held by the speakers; (6) the topic and comments; (7) the types of events: e.g. questions, commands, jokes.

Subject selection

Investigators selected the study sample after visiting three bilingual classes in the Chicago area. Classrooms were observed in terms of program structure, availability of children and teacher co-operation as well as physical environment. Nineteen children from two classrooms were selected as potential subjects for the study. The purpose of the subject selection was to find children of Hispanic origin at each of six different levels of Spanish and English proficiencies:

1. High English Proficiency — High Spanish Proficiency
2. High English Proficiency — Low Spanish Proficiency
3. High English Prociency — No Spanish Proficiency
4. Low English Proficiency — Low Spanish Proficiency
5. Low English Proficiency — High Spanish Proficiency
6. No English Proficiency — High Spanish Proficiency

The degrees of proficiency used are the ones described by De Avila & Duncan (1977) in the *Language Assessment Scales* (*LAS*). These descriptions appear in, and apply to both Spanish and English.

The language proficiency of the possible target children was determined by 4 criteria: a) administration of the LAS in both Spanish and English; b) rating of proficiency levels (in both languages) by the researchers after interviewing each child; c) the teacher's perception of each child's language proficiency in both Spanish and English; and the parents' perception of their own children's proficiency level in Spanish and English. The list of target children was narrowed down by choosing only children where at least three out of these four criteria were in agreement on the child's proficiency level. As much as possible, the subjects selected for the study came from the same classroom, same ethnic background and were of the same age and sex. Table 1 shows the breakdown of the subjects by sex and ethnicity.

TABLE 1 *Subjects. Breakdown by proficiency in Spanish and English, sex and ethnicity*

Subject	Proficiency description	Female	Male
1	High English — High Spanish	Mexican	
2	High English — Low Spanish	Mexican/Puerto Rican	
3	High English — No Spanish	Mexican/Puerto Rican	
4	Low English — Low Spanish		Mexican
5	Low English — High Spanish	Mexican	
6	No English — High Spanish		Puerto Rican

All the subjects selected were between 8.6 and 9.6 years of age and were attending third grade. Subjects 1, 2 and 3 had lived in the U.S.A. all their lives while all the others had immigrated or migrated to the U.S. within the last six years (range from six months to five years). Before the subjects were finally selected for the study, parents signed a written permission agreeing to allow their children to be videotaped in different settings.

Home background of subjects

Subject 1: Paula, who is proficient in both Spanish and English, was born in California. She lives with her parents and older brother. Her mother reports oral and reading ability in English and Spanish. They usually speak more Spanish than English at home and prefer to listen to radio or to watch television in English. They live in an integrated white-Hispanic, low socio-economic status (SES) neighborhood.

Subject 2: Ana is proficient in English and shows low proficiency in Spanish, she was born in Waukegan, Illinois, lives in a low middle-class, white neighborhood with her mother and a younger brother (age three). She speaks mainly English at home. She practises Spanish when she visits her grandmother who lives in town.

Subject 3: Carmen is proficient in English but shows almost no proficiency in Spanish. She was born in Waukegan where she lives with her mother and stepfather in a low middle-class white neighborhood. She has an older sister and a younger brother. She spoke mainly English at home until her mother remarried someone who spoke only Spanish. The mother now wants Carmen to participate in the bilingual class so that she can learn and practise Spanish in order to better communicate with her stepfather.

Subject 4: José who has low proficiency in both languages, was born in Mexico. He came to the U.S.A. about five years ago. He has older siblings to whom he speaks mainly Spanish. His parents, who work full time, report that they listen to the radio or watch television predominantly in Spanish. Their house, which they own, is situated in an integrated neighborhood.

Subject 5: Juanita has been in the U.S.A. less than a year and is highly proficient in Spanish but not so in English. She has younger siblings. The grandmother lives with them at home. The parents report that they speak only Spanish to their children. They live in a low SES neighborhood composed mainly of Hispanics and whites.

Subject 6: César has been on the U.S. mainland less than a year and like Juanita has high Spanish proficiency but low English proficiency. He lives with his mother, who speaks only Spanish, and two older siblings who are learning English. The mother reports that she has no proficiency in English and that she has an elementary school educational background. At home they prefer to listen to radio or to watch television in Spanish. The family lives in a low SES, mixed, Hispanic-Black neighborhood.

Subjects' teacher

The teacher in the class chosen for the study is an Anglo female, born in South America to missionary parents. She has a good command of Spanish, and has taught elementary school for two years. She is very organized (as reflected in her classroom management techniques and in her workplans) and committed to her teaching.

Although the classroom was structured, it was run in a relaxed manner where the children could interact not only with the teacher but with other children during the different activities. The class was conducted predominantly in English, although the teacher would often translate for the non-English speaking children, especially to give explanations and/or directions. The teacher taught Spanish to the whole class three times a week, so most children knew some Spanish, and the English speaking children were helpful to those learning English.

The teacher had an aide who was Puerto Rican, dominant in Spanish and with a good command of English, although she spoke it with a strong accent. The teacher aide was in charge of the four children who had low English proficiency. She was to give them special help in the areas of Spanish and English reading and language arts, as well as to assist them with worksheet assignments in different areas.

Data collection

Videotaped data on each child were collected. The researchers observed the classroom, became familiar with the children and visited their homes before undertaking formal videotaping. Field notes were collected at these times. Parents of the subjects as well as three groups of 25 people from the Hispanic community, each pertaining to three different age groups (three generations), were interviewed in order to determine their language use patterns and their attitudes toward language, school, etc. Afterwards, each child was videotaped with a stationary Sony AVC 3250 camera during one school day. Each target child wore a lapel microphone during the taping session. A wireless microphone was tried at first but problems with frequency interruptions made it ultimately impossible to use for data collection purposes. The camera was focused on the target child and the children around her or him.

Subsequently, children were videotaped at home, playing with other children and at a picnic where all six children were able to interact. Several audio recorders were used to collect data in areas where the camera was not recording. Furthermore, the parents were audio-recorded during the interview in order to collect sample parent language data.

Data analysis

A transcription code system was developed to analyze the videotaped data. The information coded included the following:

1. Location of interaction or utterances (in the case of soliloquia);
2. Speaker: TC=target child, AC=another child, T=teacher, Exp=experimenter;
3. Transcription (only conversations in which the target child was involved were transcribed);
4. Context (information relative to the lesson, activity, etc.);
5. Immediate situation (a brief description of what is happening between people involved in the interaction);
6. Translation (if in Spanish).

The transcription system was explained to several assistants who transcribed the tapes. A researcher was available to clear up any ambiguity. Subsequently, a different assistant checked the same tape to assure the reliability and validity of the information.

A system to code target children interactions was designed using the information obtained from the transcripts. An *interaction* was defined as a series of conversational turns by two or more speakers around a common activity or topic which are temporarily related. A listing of these interactions per child forms the language repertoire for the study. For this chapter *only* the school language repertoire is discussed.

The language repertoire of each child was quantified according to the number of utterances. Utterances are defined as units of speech (sentences, phrases, words) which express an idea and/or intent. Utterances, may be just one word or may be very complex sentences in form and/or function and, as such, do not reflect the same degree of proficiency.

As shown in Tables 2 and 3, the Spanish and English utterances for each child were counted per subject and language and per subject and setting. It is important to clarify that the number of total utterances is not a measure of language proficiency in Spanish and English. However, it is expected that a child who is more proficient in English will produce more utterances in English than Spanish and vice versa. For bilingual children it should be noted, the language used in an interaction will depend upon the situation, the context, the interlocutor, etc., involved in the interaction.

TABLE 2 *Students' language repertoire per subject and language*

| | | Utterances | | |
| | | % | % | % |
Subject	Total	English	Spanish	Mix
Paula	874	64.5	33.5	1.0
Carmen	603	96.7	2.7	.6
Ana	535	94.5	5.4	–
José	393	18.4	80.4	1.2
Juanita	1143	13.0	84.7	2.3
César	653	16.5	83.1	.4

TABLE 3 *Students' language repertoire per language and setting*

	English			Spanish		
Subject	Total Utterances	% Home*	% School	Total Utterances	% Home	% School
Paula	676	50.1	49.9	187	93.5	6.4
Carmen	591	54.3	45.7	120	90	10.0
Ana	468	44.4	55.6	68	17.6	82.3†
José	103	44.7	55.3	284	70.8	29.2
Juanita	167	74.3	25.7	941	86.0	14.0
César*	99	76.8	23.2	527	72.7	27.3

Note: *Home language was collected mainly from play activities with siblings and/or friends.
†Ana's Spanish repertoire at school includes a 15 minute talk with one of the researchers. The conversation was all in Spanish and most of Ana's responses in Spanish were one word utterances (vocabulary items).

Two hundred and fifty-six questions were used by the six children. A taxonomy used to describe the students' questions was based on available studies (Ervin-Tripp & Mitchell-Kernan, 1977) and on personal observation. Table 4 lists the types, definitions, and examples of questions employed by the children. It can be noted from this table that the children's repertoire of questions goes beyond simple requests for information — as questions are generally considered — to requests for action, to imbedded imperatives, and to rhetorical questions. The data were coded independently by two experienced coders to assure inter-rater reliability.

A quantitative analysis of the data (Tables 4 and 5) demonstrates that, in general, questions occur more often in the language in which the children are more proficient. Furthermore, there is no significant difference in the number of questions used by each child.

TABLE4 *Repertoire of questions and examples of communicative intentions and their meaning.*

Requests for Information	solicit information about the identity, location, time or property of an object, event or situation: e.g. ¿En cuàl página vas tú?
Requests for clarification	solicit more specific information when the child has failed to understand the referent of the previous utterance; a reason or explanation; e.g. Which one?
Requests for approval	to request a judgement or an attitude about events or situations; e.g. Do you thing this looks good?
Requests for action	solicit the listener to perform, not to perform, or to stop to perform an action; e.g. José, ¿préstama esta goma?
Requests for permission	solicit permission to perform an action; e.g. Miss Jones, can I finish this?
Yes/No questions	solicit affirmation or negation of the propositional content of the addressor's utterance; e.g. Are we leaving now?
Rhetorical questions	solicit a listener's acknowledgment to allow speaker to continue; e.g. ¿Tú sabes cuántas malas me saqué?
Hesitation questions	answer a question with another question, showing hesitation and insecurity; e.g. Here . . . living room?

Discussion

Requests for information were the types of questions that had the highest frequency of occurrence in English (52.7%) as well as in Spanish (50%), followed by yes/no questions (23.6% for Spanish and 12% for English). Requests for permission and for clarification had a higher incidence of occurrence among children who were more proficient in English.

At the same time, there was a tendency to group those students who were equally proficient in both languages with English monolingual students. This was the case with Paula, the most balanced bilingual of the group, who was always assigned the same work as the English monolinguals. It may have been that her opportunities to maintain and improve her Spanish proficiency were curtailed while she continued to develop her proficiency in English. More data obtained in other, more natural settings need to be examined in order to be able to determine the types of questions

TABLE *Number and percentage of questions asked per child in the classroom*

SPANISH

Child	Paula		Juanita		César		José		Ana		Carmen		Total number of questions used by all children	
Level	5		5		5		3		2		1			
	Total use: 2		Total use: 49		Total use: 67		Total use: 39		Total use: 0		Total use: 0		Total use 159	
Occurrences and percent	Occ.	%	Occ.	%	Occ.	%	Occ.	%	Occ.	%	Occ.	%	Occ.	%
Req. info.	–	–	29	59.2	33	47.8	13	33.3	–	–	–	–	75	47.2
Req. clarif.	–	–	2	4.1	4	5.8	10	25.6	–	–	–	–	16	10.1
Req. permis	–	–	1	2.0	2	2.9	–	–	–	–	–	–	3	1.9
Req. approv.	–	–	2	4.1	6	8.7	4	10.3	–	–	–	–	12	7.5
Yes/No ques.	2	100	13	26.5	21	30.4	3	7.7	–	–	–	–	39	24.4
Req. action	–	–	–	–	3	4.4	7	17.9	–	–	–	–	10	6.3
Rhet. ques.	–	–	–	–	–	–	2	5.2	–	–	–	–	2	1.3
Hesi. ques.	–	–	2	4.1	–	–	–	–	–	–	–	–	2	1.3

TABLE 6 *Number and percentage of questions asked per child in the classroom*

ENGLISH

Child	Paula		Ana		Carmen		José		Juanita		César		Total number of questions used by all children	
Level	5		5		5		3		1–2		1			
	Total use: 52		Total use: 58		Total use: 54		Total use: 11		Total use: 1		Total use: 3		Total use 179	
Occurrences and percent	Occ.	%	Occ.	%	Occ.	%	Occ.	%	Occ.	%	Occ.	%	Occ.	%
Req. info.	17	32.7	22	37.9	26	48.1	3	27.3	1	100	1	35.3	70	39.1
Req. clarif.	3	5.8	13	22.4	7	13	3	27.3	–	–	–	–	26	14.5
Req. permis.	–	–	11	19	8	14.8	–	–	–	–	1	35.3	20	11.2
Req. approv.	1	1.9	–	–	4	7.4	–	–	–	–	–	–	5	2.8
Yes/No ques.	10	19.2	9	15.5	6	11.1	1	9.1	–	–	1	33.1	27	15.1
Req. action	3	5.8	2	3.5	–	–	–	–	–	–	–	–	5	2.8
Rhet. ques.	8	15.4	1	1.7	3	5.6	–	–	–	–	–	–	12	6.7
Hesi. ques.	10	19.2	–	–	–	–	4	36.3	–	–	–	–	14	7.8

used more often by children who have low proficiency in either of the two languages.

Not all utterances were composed of full propositions. Many questions consisted of only one word requests for clarification, such as "huh?", which is a recurrent pattern in children with low proficiency. For example, this was observed with Ana when she tried to have a conversation with one of the researchers in Spanish.

Some of the questions were ambiguous. Yes/no questions seemed similar on certain occasions to requests for approval, and requests for information could also have been coded as imbedded imperatives. After looking at the context it was found that the question was a request for action by the addressee, as in the following example:

César: ¿Tienes lápiz grande?
(*Do you have a big pencil?*) (Waits for pencil)
Préstaselo a José.
(*Lend it to José*).
Arturo: No sabía que eras su amigo tantito.
(*I didn't know you were his friend.*)
César: Tantico nomas. Préstaselo pa'cer el work y más na.
(*Just for a few minutes. Let him use it to work and nothing else.*)

Rhetorical questions seem to be a more sophisticated level of language use. The majority of the rhetorical questions were in English and were used by students who had a high level of proficiency in that language, e.g.

Paula: These are my pencils.
Mimi: One is mine
Paula: That's . . . How am I going to erase them?
Mimi, could I have your eraser?

It is obvious in the preceding example that the addresser does not expect to get an answer to her question (How am I going to erase them?) and thus she continues with the next request for action. An interesting kind of discourse pattern occurs when questions are used to answer other questions because speakers do not want to commit themselves to a definite answer, e.g.

T: How would you feel about this friend of yours telling your teacher?
Paula: Sad?
T: What would you want to do with that friend?
Paula: Beat him?

These types of answers are particularly noticeable in the speech of José a very low English proficient speaker when he tries to communicate in that language, e.g.

T: José, tell me where are these people going to sleep
José: Here . . . living room?
T: Okay. No, in the bedroom.

T: Where did you put your milk?
José: In here.
T: What's that?
José: The refrigerator?

José's hesitation and insecurity in answering in English was increased by the attitude of the teacher who often ignored his questions and continued to speak without paying attention to him. Furthermore, he did not seem to be accepted by the rest of his classmates who felt that his Spanish discourse relied too heavily on lexical items which they did not consider appropriate for classroom interactions. They would regularly laugh at him when he made mistakes. This contributed to his feeling of insecurity and to his hesitating questions, e.g.

T: But this here is a rug. It's on the . . .
José: Rug? (Everybody laughs, José looks embarrassed.)
T: It's on the floor. The rug is on the floor.

Although Paula would also sometimes hesitate in discourse, her answers did not produce the same derisive reaction as José's. This difference seemed to occur because Paula was a leader in the class and had high proficiency in both languages.

It should be pointed out that some of the children may have asked questions of a certain type only in one of the two languages because of the classroom structure. The limited English proficient (LEP) students in this sample were, perhaps, involuntarily isolated from the more English proficient students because they often worked in small group situations with the teacher aide where the interaction tended to be in Spanish. Even when the groups were reading in English, the children asked the teacher aide questions in Spanish to which she also replied in Spanish.

The data demonstrates that the same types of questions are asked in both languages, although children who are more proficient in English seem to have access to a greater variety of questioning strategies. In addition, the type of setting or activity seems to influence the language in which the questions are asked. Consequently, in a bilingual class, in order for the children to grow proficient in two languages they need to be given an opportunity to work in different groups so that they are not involuntarily isolated from a richer language experience.

In a larger study with different contexts it may be possible to demonstrate that some types of questions could be specific to certain levels of proficiency in English or Spanish. If so, this could be the basis for a construct aimed at determining language proficiency from a discourse analysis perspective. This construct would have to take into account the child's entire communicative competence rather than concentrating only on limited aspects of language competence (vocabulary, grammar), which are usually based on adults' expectations of children's linguistic performance.

Conclusion

The purpose of the paper was to show that children who are at different levels of language proficiency possess a rich repertoire of interrogative forms. Questions are used in classroom interactions in order to communicate various messages, such as requests for information, requests for action, or requests for permission. Questions are most often employed in the language in which the child is more proficient, and the questions are often determined by the type of setting or activity in which the children participate.

It appears that when the language repertoire of children is analyzed from an integrative perspective, a better description of the children's communicative competence is possible. By looking for what adults feel children should know, educators have been disregarding children's actual performance.

New studies in child discourse across levels may open new avenues for testing language constructs which are integrative and holistic, and which take into account form as well as functions of language. In this way, a better understanding of the communicative competence of bilingual children may be gained.

References

Blom, J. P. & Gumperz, J. J. 1972, Social meaning in linguistic structure: Code-switching in Norway. In J. J. Gumperz & D. Hymes (eds), *Directions in sociolinguistics*. New York: Holt, Rinehart, and Winston, 407–34.

Coulthard, R. M. 1977, *An introduction to discourse analysis*. London: Longman.

De Avila, E. & Duncan, S. E. 1977, *Language assessment scales* (2nd. ed.), Corte Madera, CA: Linguametrics Group.

Dore, J. 1977, "Oh them sheriff": A pragmatic analysis of chidren's responses to questions. In S. Ervin-Tripp & C. Mitchell-Kernan (eds), *Child discourse*. New York: Academic Press, 139–63.

Ervin-Tripp, Susan 1977, Wait for me, Roller Skate! In S. Ervin-Tripp and C. Mitchell-Kernan (eds), *Child Discourse*. New York: Academic Press, pp. 165–88.

Ervin-Tripp, S. & Mitchell-Kernan, C. (eds), 1977, *Child discourse*. New York: Academic Press.

González, G. 1970, *The acquisition of Spanish grammar by native Spanish speakers*. Unpublished doctoral dissertation, University of Texas.

Gumperz, J. J. 1964, Linguistic and social interaction in two communities. *American Anthropologist*, 66(6) (Pt. 2), 137–53.

Hernández-Chàvez, E. 1978, Critique of a critique: Issues in language assessment. *NABE Journal*, 11(2), 47–56.

Hymes, D. 1971, Sociolinguistics and the enthnography of speaking. In E. Ardener (ed.), *Social Anthropology and Language*. London: Tavistock, 47–93.

— 1974, *Foundations in sociolinguistics: An ethnographic approach*. Philadelphia: University of Pennsylvania Press.

Labov, W. 1966, *The social stratification of English in New York City*. Washington, D.C.: Center for Applied Linguistics.

— 1972, Roles for ritual insults. In D. Sudnow (ed.), *Studies in social interaction*. New York: Free Press, 120–69.

Lance, D. M. 1975, Dialectal and nonstandard forms in Texas Spanish. In E. Hernández-Chávez *et al.* (eds), *El lenguaje de los Chicanos: Regional and social characteristics of language used by Mexican Americans*. Arlington, VA: Center for Applied Linguistics, 37–51.

Lavandera, B. 1978, The variable component in bilingual performance. In J. E. Alatis (ed.), *29th Georgetown University Round Table on Languages and Linguistics: International dimensions of bilingual education*. Washington, D.C.: Georgetown University Press, 391–410.

McClure, E. G. 1977, *Aspects of code-switching in the discourse of bilingual Mexican-American Children* (Tech. Rep. 44). Champaign, Illinois: Center for the Study of Reading.

Peñalosa, F. 1979, *Chicano sociolinguistics: A brief introduction*. Rowley, Mass.: Newbury House.

Poplack, S. 1979, *Sometimes I'll start a sentence in Spanish Y TERMINO EN ESPAÑOL: Toward a typology of code-switching*. New York: Centro de Estudios Puertorriqueños.

Shuy, R. W. 1977, Quantitative language data: A case for and some warnings against. *Anthropology and Education*, 8(2), 73–82.

Sinclair, J. & Coulthard, R. M. 1975, *Towards an analysis of discourse: The English used by teachers and pupils*. London: Oxford University Press.

Zentella, A. C. 1978, Code-switching and interactions among Puerto Rican children. *Working Papers in Sociolinguistics* (No. 50). Austin, Texas: Southwest Educational Development Laboratory.

Intergenerational variation in language use and structure in a bilingual context[1]

Shana Poplack
Center for Puerto Rican Studies
City University of New York and University of Ottawa

The structure of the vernacular cannot be meaningfully studied through the introspection, elicitation and grammaticality/acceptability test data ordinarily used by linguists. An internalized normativity based on the "standard" language irretrievably biases all such data. Choices of register, style and other aspects of discourse mode are equally difficult to assess systematically through introspection, since such choices are most often not the result of conscious conversational strategy, and, as long as they are situationally appropriate choices, are not even noticed by speaker or hearer. Nor does the native speaker's faculty for grammatical judgement apply here in the same way it does to phonological strings or syntactic constructions.

These two types of problems are compounded in the study of bilingualism in a minority community. Consider first the structural level. Not only is the minority variety of the majority language usually very highly stigmatized, but also the minority language itself characteristically shows many signs of adaptation to the bilingual situation. These changes are typically rejected and denied by even the more progressive community members. Reliance on elicitation or grammaticality judgements is notoriously misleading in such a situation. But since even observation depends on access to very specific naturalistic conditions, and these conditions are not compatible with the presence of a scientific observer, much research on bilingual grammar has been based on testing and elicitation in artificial conditions, often leading to spurious results.

Turning from the structural to the interactional level, we find that this sensitivity to context also leads to severe difficulties in studying the choice and functions of various discourse modes, precisely because bilinguals' choice of language or their use of code-switching become key elements in their repertoire of discourse modes. This is reflected in the pervasiveness of interpretivist analyses of language choice among scholars of bilingualism. Since the Observer's Paradox makes it so difficult to obtain naturalistic data, systematic and predictive studies are beyond the resources of most researchers, and so attention is focused on the occasional example of unexpected choice of language or code-switch in an attempt to infer its interactional significance or symbolic role in conversation. These studies, though often very insightful, can only serve to furnish initial hypotheses about the special nature of bilingual interaction within the community.

In this chapter I stress the role of long-term participant observation as part of an interdisciplinary approach to resolving these problems in the study of bilingualism. On the interactional level, this provides the critical check on self-report, attitudinal data and test results. The contrast between the latter types of elicited information and observations of naturally occurring behavior leads to a much clearer understanding of patterns of language use and the sociological and ideological forces which mold these patterns. It allows one to make inferences about the current evolution of language choice with far more accuracy and confidence than questioning or test results could afford.

For studies on the structural level, the use made of the ethnographic contribution is very specific and limited in nature, but nonetheless indispensable. The role of ethnography in the sociolinguistic studies reported in ensuing sections was primarily to provide contextually validated data in quantities large enough for input into the quantitative analysis of structural variation. The stress on natural context is crucial to obtaining authentic data on, for example, code-switching, which has been shown to be virtually unobtainable using other methodologies (Poplack, 1981). Thus the participant observation effectively opens up a class of entirely new possibilities for analyses of bilingual grammar. This is not, however, the primary goal of the ethnographic component of the study, nor is the quantity and quality of data obtained in this way capable, in and of itself, of providing answers to the specific questions we have raised regarding the effects of language contact without first undergoing rigorous linguistic and statistical analysis to clarify and confirm the nature of variation and change within the community.

In what follows, I document the results of a series of studies of language use in a stable bilingual Puerto Rican community. These studies illustrate the utility of an interdisciplinary approach to the assessment of bilingual linguistic competence.

In a first set of studies (Language Policy Task Force, 1980) long-term participant observation was used, along with detailed attitude questionnaires and quantitative sociolinguistic analyses of selected linguistic features in order to ascertain: whether Spanish was being maintained among the adults in the community; their feelings regarding maintenance or loss; and, whether and how the variety of Spanish spoken had been affected by close contact with English.

All the ninety-one individuals in the sample were found to be bilingual to some degree, ranging from passive knowledge of one of the two languages involved, to full productive competence in both, skills which for the most part, had been acquired outside of any formal language instruction. Though community members were well aware of the negative attitudes of outsiders towards Puerto Rican varieties of Spanish (and English), they generally assessed their Spanish as "good". And indeed, quantitative sociolinguistic analyses of morphological, syntactic and semantic aspects of Puerto Rican Spanish (Poplack, 1982) reveal not only that fundamental differences between this variety and the so-called "standard" are very limited, but also that differences which do emerge are intra-systemic and cannot be accounted for merely by recourse to the explanation of contact with English.

One finding which may appear not to favor the maintenance of Spanish in this community is the observation that neither Spanish nor English is used exclusively in any domain (Pedraza, 1981). Such functional separation of languages has been considered necessary (e.g. Fishman, 1966) for the survival of the subordinate language. Nonetheless, the overwhelming majority of adults (about 90%) want their children to speak Spanish as a first language (most parents in fact want their children to acquire both simultaneously), a responsibility very few place on the schools. Rather the consensus seems to be that all sectors — school, family and community — contribute to the maintenance of Spanish (Language Policy Task Force, 1980). However, these same ethnographic observations suggested that most younger Puerto Ricans of the third generation prefer English, a finding which could be interpreted as evidence of language shift. This raised the question of how the community language skills, attitudes and use were transmitted from one generation to the next.

A subsequent series of studies focused on language distribution among the children in the community, using the same three-faceted methodology described above. The goal was to find out whether English was in fact gaining among these youngsters, and the nature of the competing roles of family, community and school in affecting maintenance, shift or loss. Labov's studies of Black English Vernacular among South Harlem adolescent peer-groups had already demonstrated the primacy of peer influence over parental linguistic patterns (Labov, 1972; Labov, Cohen, Robins & Lewis, 1968). Labov has also detailed the microsociological implications of the conflicting norms represented by peers vs. schools and the wider society. The alternating use of Spanish and English among Puerto Rican children is subject to these same three sources of external influence — the home, the school and the peer group in the community. Here, however, the situation is somewhat more complex. For example, what would be the effect of a monolingual Spanish home environment and mainly English peer involvement on the current and future language preference of a child? How does enrolment in monolingual English vs. bilingual school programs cross-cut or reinforce these competing influences?

Data and methods

The research on language distribution among the children in the community is based on data collected from sixteen Puerto Rican children ranging in age from five to twelve years. The sample was chosen fo fit the following criteria:

1. In order to investigate the inter-generational transmission of bilingual skills the children were offspring of adults already studied;
2. In order to compare the effects on language structure and language choice of monolingual vs. bilingual education programs they attended P.S. 222, a local elementary school with a bilingual program;
3. They were either of school entry age (Kindergarten through second grade), when home influence on language choice is greatest, or leaving elementary school (grades five and six), when peer influence is presumably stronger.

These children were observed for nearly two years in their classrooms, in the lunchroom and at recess. During the summer holidays the children were followed back to the block and observed on the street interacting with their peers and at home with their families. They were also tape-recorded in all these situations as well as more formal ones, (i.e. responses to a language attitude survey, replies to a semi-formal "sociolinguistic interview", and various psycholinguistic tests of language dominance). This yielded a very large data base, consisting of observations of language use in all these settings, the children's own reports and attitudes toward their language use (as emerged from their responses to the formal instruments), and 165 hours of tape-recorded speech as actually used in each setting.

Intergenerational aspects of language use

All but one of the children's parents claim Spanish as their "first" language; almost all consider it their current "stronger" language, despite having been in the United States anywhere from two to forty-seven years. The older generation is equally divided between those who report using exclusively Spanish with all interactants (parents, siblings, peers, children and co-workers where applicable), and those who report using both languages depending on the interlocutor. This is in sharp contrast to their children, none of whom report using only Spanish with all interactants. Indeed, two thirds of the children claimed *no* interactant or setting which required exclusively Spanish. This can be seen in Figure 1.

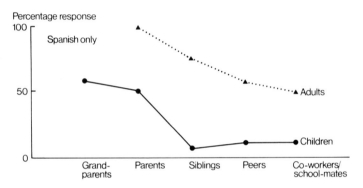

FIGURE 1 *Reported use of Spanish only by adults and children according to the interlocutor*

The data in Figure 1 appear to suggest the use of only Spanish as a function of familial relationships and generational distance. The graph shows that use of Spanish is perceived to decrease from family members to non-family members, and within the family from the older generation to siblings.

But the difference between the number of parents and children who report using only Spanish appears from Figure 1 to be very great, and if we were to limit the analysis to this figure alone, we would have to conclude that use of Spanish is decreasing rapidly among the younger generation; whereas *all* of the adults report using exclusively Spanish with their parents, no more than 58% of the children speak only Spanish with their grandparents. Indeed, parents and grandparents are the sole interactants with whom more than half of the children report speaking only Spanish, an assessment which coincides exactly with what their own parents report.

However, examination of Figure 2 shows that sole use of English with various interlocutors is reported by fewer than one third of both parents and children; if anything, by fewer children than adults. The key difference between the parents and the children lies in the number of children who report using *both* languages with the interactants in question (Figure 3). Indeed, it is in interactions with siblings that most respondents claim to use both Spanish and English. In particular, it appears from these figures that interactions which were carried out by the older generation solely or predominantly in Spanish (especially those involving parents and siblings) are now reported by the younger generation to be carried out in both.[2] This is to be expected from the nature of the community in which these children were born and raised (Language Policy Task Force, 1980), where there are only very few completely monolingual speakers of either language. Yet it is

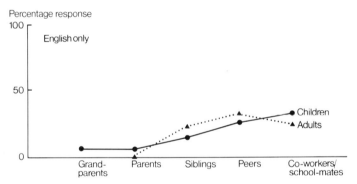

FIGURE 2 *Reported use of English only by adults and children according to interlocutor*

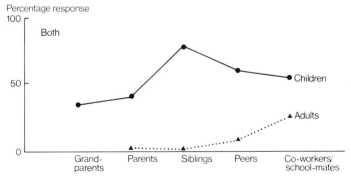

FIGURE 3 *Reported use of both Spanish and English by adults and children according to interlocutor.*

also the case that children are responsible for introducing English into previously all-Spanish domains, a finding which may be interpreted in favor of language shift (e.g. Fishman, 1966; Cornejo, 1973; Gal, 1978), which in turn, according to the paradigm espoused by many studies, should lead to language loss. Observations of language use in the three settings of home, school and block, however, reveal that the factors affecting language choice are far more complex and varied than simple reports of language use according to one's interlocutor would indicate. They clearly demonstrate that in a sociolinguistically complex, stable bilingual community, even one as ethnically and socio-economically homogeneous as the one under investigation, no single factor, be it migratory history, familial linguistic preference, school program or personal attitude, is sufficient, in and of itself, to account completely for the language usage of its individual members.

Competing influences on current language preference

A major goal of this work was to discover which domain — home, school or peer/block — would prove most influential in cases of conflict. Close observation, however, reveals that the very nature of these environments allows for differential degrees of freedom of language choice.[3] A combination of factors makes the influence of the home crucial to language choice among Puerto Rican children. Parents control the linguistic exposure the child receives within the home via choice of guests, television and radio programs, etc. Parents are also ultimately responsible for an even more influential factor in determining language preference — permitting the child the freedom to come and go outside the home and thus indirectly allowing him/her to come under influences other than familial. Finally, the factor of *respeto*, which requires accommodating to the (linguistic and other) desires of one's elders, is clearly at play as well (Pedraza, 1981). Within the home, then, a child appears to enjoy only limited freedom of language choice: Spanish, either alone, or in conjunction with English, is the most appropriate option in this setting.

In comparison with the situation in a child's home, the use of language in the classroom is correctly perceived as far more strongly constrained by an influence exterior to the child's own will: the teacher. Observation showed that in class, language selection was consistent with the intended language allocation of the program (i.e. children in monolingual classes speak primarily English while those in bilingual classes use both languages, depending on the task at hand).

With peers on the block, in contrast, apart from a limited number of generalized, community-wide norms for language use,[4] a child is free to use either Spanish or English or both, largely because models for all of these are provided by the adults in the community, who carry out a large part of their social interaction in public. Choice of language in this domain is thus the most sensitive indicator of the child's overall linguistic preference.

Long-term observation of interaction on the block provides evidence in turn of a complex relationship between language use, peer interaction patterns and sex of the interactant.

Table 1 shows that those children who by choice or compulsion are

TABLE 1 *Observed language received at home and used overall, along with school program placement for "lame" and "streetwise" children*

	"Lame"		
	Home language[a]	Language used most in all settings	School program
Girls:			
Iris	S[b]	S	B
Josie	B	B	B
Dorcas	B	B	B
Debbie	B	E	E
Linda	E	E	E
Boys:			
Pito	E	E	E
Herminio	S	S	B
	"Streetwise"		
	Home language	Language used most in all settings	School program
Girls:			
Juanita	S	B	B
Flaquita	S	B	B
Maria	B	B	E
Boys:			
Chico	S	S	B
Gordito	B	E	E
Baby	S	E	E
Ramón	B	E	E
Indio	S	E	B
Conejo	S	E	B

[a] Language received at home.

[b] Designation refers to language used most frequently.
E = English, S = Spanish, B = both or Bilingual.

isolated from their peers (whom we have designated "lames") show an overall preference for the language of the home (which in turn correlates perfectly with their placement in a particular school program). For those who are "streetwise" (i.e. have extensive peer contact and freedom of movement both on and off the block), parental influence is more diffuse, and the child's school placement does not necessarily correlate with either home language or overall preferred language. Table 1 further suggests that it is the interaction of sex with peer involvement which explains current language preference. Boys with extensive peer and block involvement tend to prefer English, regardless of home language and school placement. Boys who are more isolated, on the other hand, speak the language of the home, whichever it may be. In contrast, girls (streetwise *or* lame) tend to use both languages (unless their home environments are overwhelmingly monolingual, in which case they prefer the language of the home).

The factors affecting language distribution among children basically correspond to larger community norms, except that children appear to be subject to a higher standard of expectation than adults: it is generally taken for granted that children are English speakers, yet they are also (explicitly or implicitly) expected to maintain Spanish.

Reported vs. Observed language use

Next examined in detail are differences between reported and observed language use in the three domains of home, school and block, as in Table 2. The starred letters on the right indicate disagreements between reported and observed assessment.

As Table 2 illustrates, most of the children report themselves to adapt their linguistic behavior to the setting (e.g. they report some differentiation among language choice specific to home, school and/or block), indicating a perceived separation of language choice by domain. However, our observations show the opposite situation — in only a few cases does language preference change according to domain, paralleling in this regard what had already been found for the adult members of the community.

When comparing reports with observations for children placed in bilingual as opposed to monolingual classes, a number of points emerge. We first note that one third of the reports disagree with the observations. This is actually a surprisingly low figure considering the age of the children (some of whom were five years old at the time of the interview), and the nature of the questions, which do not take a simple yes-no answer.

Notwithstanding, comparison of children in bilingual and monolingual classes reveals some striking differences. For one thing, none of the children in monolingual (i.e. English) classes reports (nor, more strikingly, is

TABLE 2 *Reported and observed language used most frequently at home, on the block and in school according to placement in school program.*

	Reported			Observed		
	Home	Block	School	Home	Block	School
Bilingual class						
Iris	B^a	S	S	S^b*	S	S
Indio	B	E	B	B	E	B
Conejo	S	B	B	B*	E*	B
Juanita	B	B	E	B	B	B*
Flaquita	B	B	B	B	B	B
Josie	B	E	B	B	B*	B
Dorcas	B	B	B	B	B	B
Chico	B	S	S	S*	S	S
Herminio	B	B	B	S*	S*	B
Monolingual class						
María	B	B	B	B	B	B
Pito	E	E	E	E	E	E
Debbie	B	E	E	E*	E	E
Ramón	B	B	B	E*	E*	E*
Gordito	B	B	E	B	E*	E
Linda	B	B	E	E*	E*	E

^a Designations refers to language used most frequently.
  E = English, S = Spanish, B = both or Bilingual.
^b Starred letters indicate a discrepancy in reported and observed language use.

observed) using predominantly Spanish in any of the three domains. This is in contrast to five reports of Spanish-only use (out of a possible twenty-seven) from those in bilingual classes, and eight of twenty-seven observations of exclusive Spanish use. However, interestingly enough, disagreements between report and observation among children in monolingual classes show a consistent pattern of over-rating Spanish use. More than one third of the reports (seven out of eighteen) indicated use of both languages, particularly at home and on the block (where half of the reports did not coincide for both domains), while observation indicated predominant use of English. This is understandable in view of the favored status of home and block for Spanish use discussed above.

The discrepancies between reports and observations among children in bilingual classes show a tendency in the opposite direction noted for the monolinguals: either over-rating their English or under-rating their Spanish (i.e. reporting more use of both languages when they were actually observed to use Spanish). These differences may be explicable in terms of the children's attitudes.

In response to questions attempting to tap attitudes towards Spanish such as: "Would you like to speak better Spanish than you do?"; "If someone said you talked like a Puerto Rican, would that make you feel good?"; and "Do you think a Puerto Rican kid should know how to speak Spanish?", the responses from the children in monolingual programs were overwhelmingly favorable. Responses from those in bilingual classes were somewhat more noncommital. Children in monolingual classes apparently like to think of themselves as using more Spanish than they actually do, while the reverse appears to be true of those for whom Spanish is more commonplace.

Having examined the children's control of appropriateness norms according to interlocutor and setting, we next investigate how being brought up in a stable bilingual community has affected the linguistic structure of their communicative behavior. These studies, which focus on the way English influences have or have not affected the structure of Spanish, are carried out against a background of extensive studies of adults in the same community, and deal with phenomena which are *not* taught in either bilingual or monolingual classes.

We have seen above that the net effect of demographic movements and conflicting sociological forces is to expand the domains of appropriateness of English, apparently without, however, shrinking the functional range of Spanish. Thus many contexts in which both languages are used were observed. This is the type of situation in which scholars and intellectuals have perceived the greatest danger to the integrity of the minority language, citing processes such as borrowing from English and code-switching as the mechanisms for its simplification and eventual demise (e.g. Varo, 1971; Harris, 1979). It has been shown that many of these perceptions are overgeneralizations or sterotypes based on impressions and anecdotes (Poplack, 1982). To reach a genuine understanding of the nature of the effect, if any, English is exercising on the Spanish spoken by these children, it is first necessary to ascertain through participant observation, that the data represent authentic and naturalistic linguistic usage in context; and then attempt to assess objectively and empirically the nature and amount of influence, using rigorous linguistic and statistical criteria.

The introduction and integration of loanwords

In the course of classroom observation and other parts of the ethnographic investigation, the use of various English words in otherwise Spanish context was noted. These were assumed to be potential loanwords. However, few of these words occurred more than once or twice, largely because the particular topics of conversation which gave rise to them were seldom repeated. Thus the observational data on each word were insufficient for any systematic analysis. Accordingly, in a study of the introduction and incorporation of borrowed material into Puerto Rican Spanish (Poplack & Sankoff, 1980) designations of forty-five objects, or types of objects, were elicited from fourteen of the children in the sample and their parents. The goal was threefold: 1) to examine the mechanics of borrowing, and in particular the linguistic processes by which words are incorporated ("integrated") into the lexicon of the recipient language; 2) to contribute to the development of criteria for deciding: when insertion into one code of items from another should be considered a bona-fide "loanword"; when it represents an instance of code-switching; and, when we may be justified in speaking of "interference"; and finally, 3) to empirically investigate a number of current claims in the literature regarding the social dynamics of borrowing; in particular, the behavior of older vs. younger, and adult (non-fluent) vs. childhood (fluent) bilinguals in the adaptation of loanwords (e.g. Fries & Pike, 1949; Haugen 1950, 1956). We focus on the last of these here.

Studies of language contact have stressed two basically sociological or sociolinguistic distinctions as being relevant to the incorporation of borrowed material into the linguistic repertoire of the community. One is the differential role of monolinguals vs. bilinguals of varying degrees of competence as carriers of innovations; the other involves the changing shape of loanwords across successive generations of speakers.

A common view is that bilinguals tend to use loanwords before monolinguals, who learn them from the former. Bilingual speakers are also thought to assimilate new sounds sooner than their monolingual counterparts (Fries & Pike, 1949). Haugen (1956) distinguishes between monolinguals and those who became bilingual as adults on the one hand, and childhood bilinguals on the other.[5] Observing that borrowed items tend to retain an uncertain linguistic status for some time after their first adoption, he attributes part of this vacillation to the awareness on the part of the bilingual of the origin of the borrowed word, and presumably, to his or her indecision as to whether to produce it according to recipient or donor language rules. In addition, both monolinguals and non-fluent ("adult") bilinguals make phonic adaptations (or "distortions") of loanwords, while fluent ("childhood") bilinguals reproduce the patterns of the donor language (Haugen 1950, 1956). According to this schema, childhood bilinguals, or younger speakers, are responsible for introducing *new* patterns into the recipient language. By comparing the behavior of adults and children with regard to choice of borrowed vs. native designations, and in the case of the former, with regard to choice of phonetically, morphologically and syntactically adapted versions of the form vs. unadapted ones, we sought to ascertain whether Haugen's hypothesis also accounted for the observed variation in the Puerto Rican community.

Table 3 compares children's and adults' mean scores on twelve indices conceived to measure various aspects of the integration of English loanwords into Spanish discourse. The fact that the indices measuring the

TABLE 3 *Children's and adults' average scores on twelve indices of integration of loanwords into Spanish discourse*

Indices	Children	Adults
1. Total (Tokens)	16.5	9.2
2. Total (No Response)	0.6	0.6
3. Total (Multi-response Speakers)	4.1	1.8
4. Proportion (English Tokens)	62.6	51.2
5. Proportion (English-only Responses)	56.4	44.4
6. Proportion (Bilingual Responses)	14.3	15.2
7. Proportion (Non-Spanish Responses)	71.1	59.8
8. Proportion (English 1st Choice)	64.2	52.6
9 Proportion (English 1st Choice)	80.3	73.7
Proportion (English Tokens)		
10. Mean (Token Integration)	107.2	115.6
11. Maximum (Token Integration)	179.4	150.0
12. Gender Field Consistency	90.1	78.6

amount of English use — *Proportion (English tokens)*, *Proportion (English first choices)*, *Proportion (English-only responses)* and *Proportion (non-Spanish-only responses)* — are all higher for the children than the adults may be evidence that English usage is advancing among the younger generation, at least insofar as the semantic fields under investigation are concerned,[6] confirming the findings of the ethnographic observations presented earlier. The equivocal results for the indices measuring phonological and morphological integration of the borrowed form into Spanish patterns — children score lower on *Mean (token integration)* but higher on *Maximum (token integration)* than the adults — suggest that there is no diminishing of the Spanish phonological assimilatory mechanism in the children's speech. This would disprove contentions that there is increasing English influence in the Spanish phonology of children. It also disproves Haugen's hypothesis that childhood bilinguals (the case in varying degrees of all the children in the sample) tend to reproduce borrowed material in a form which more closely approximates that of the source language (English) than speakers who have acquired one of their two languages in adulthood.

The measures were then analyzed by means of principal components analysis, a method enabling the visualization of relationships implicit in the data by projecting a multi-dimensional data configuration down to a subspace of low dimensionality. Indices which are highly correlated are projected close together on the space spanned by the principal components, while those which are negatively correlated tend to appear far apart. Figure 4 displays the results of a principal components analysis where children's and adults' designations of the forty-five concepts are treated separately.

Without entering into detail (see Poplack & Sankoff, 1980) the indices contained in the circled area in the top right-hand quadrant of Figure 4 includes measures of English predominance over Spanish in the semantic fields under study (see key).

The two lozenge-shaped areas in the lower right-hand quadrant include measures of how well-integrated into Spanish phonological and morphological patterns are English responses to the stimuli (e.g. was the concept "mattress" designated *matre* ['matre] or *mattress* ['mætrəs]?) The remaining two circles contain measures of how many diverse designations of each stimulus were provided by the respondents (e.g. the concept "blue jeans" received eight different designations; "tape" elicited only *tape* and *cassette*). The indices GENF and genf, uncircled in the lower quadrant, measure the tendency of responses to have a consistent grammatical gender across speakers (both *el turtle* and *la térol* were offered for "turtle").

It is clear from the way the indices are disposed in the space spanned by the first two principal components that the pattern of children's responses is essentially the same as that of the adults. In fact, along the first principal component, the horizontal axis in Figure 4, there is striking congruence between the generations. In the full report of this study it is shown that this is the axis which most closely measures the overall process of loanword integration. In other words, the mechanics of integration proceed in a parallel fashion for children and adults. Insofar as there are some intergenerational differences, these are largely confined to the second principal component (the vertical axis in Figure 4), which contrasts multiple-response indices against those associated with simple responses. Here the children's indices have more extreme values than the adults', indicating a greater variability of their responses regarding the number of different terms supplied for each concept. This result is essentially an artifact of test construction, however, and does not reflect any real intergenerational linguistic difference.

One striking result to emerge from the study is the relative homogeneity

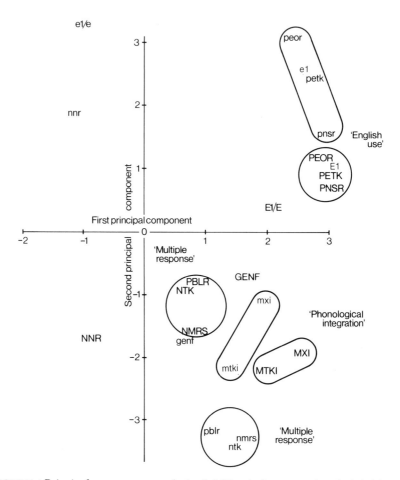

FIGURE 4 *Principal components analysis of children's (lower case) and adults' (upper case) indices: first two principal components.*

PEOR/peor = proportion of English-only responses (i.e. the proportion of speakers giving one or more responses which are all of English origin).

El/e1 = proportion of English-first-choice responses (i.e. the proportion of speakers giving an English designation first).

El/E/e1/e = proportion of English tokens which were first choices.

PETK/petk = proportion of the total number of tokens offered for a given semantic field which are identified as of English origin.

PNSR/pnsr = proportion of non-Spanish only responses (i.e. those offered in English or in English and Spanish).

PBLR/pblr = proportion of bilingual responses (i.e. the proportion of

		speakers giving at least one English and one Spanish designation).
NTK/ntk	=	Total number of answers for a given stimulus.
NMRS/nmrs	=	Number of multiple-response speakers (i.e. those who offered more than one response).
GENF/genf	=	Gender Field Consistency (i.e. the extent to which a given semantic field is consistently expressed with one gender).
MTKI/mtki	=	Mean Token Integration (i.e. the average value, over all English tokens offered for a given stimulus, of the phonological integration code for the token).
MXI/mxi	=	Maximum Token Integration (i.e. the maximum phonological integration for any English token).
NNR/nnr	=	Total (no response)

of the community with regard to loanword usage, stemming from the finding that older and younger speakers are not highly differentiated in this regard. In effect, previous hypotheses that younger speakers import phonological and morphological patterns closer to the source language were disproved. Indeed, such behavior would hardly be consistent with the very notion of speech community, as enunciated by Gumperz (1972) and Labov (1966). Rather it appears that when a term is accepted into a speech community, and adapted into a particular phonological form, it is that form which is transmitted across generations in much the same way as monolingual neologisms. This is evidence that the process of borrowing is carried out in a regular way on the community level, and is not a series of random accidents.

Gender Assignment to Borrowed Nouns

In a more detailed study of one aspect of the integration of loanwords into a recipient language system — the assignment of gender to English nouns borrowed into Spanish speech (Poplack, Pousada & Sankoff, 1982), the behavior of children and adults was again compared. Gender is a system of noun classification based on concord, whereby "gender carriers" (in Spanish, determiners, adjectives and pronouns, as well as participial verbs, under certain circumstances) must agree with the head noun, regardless of whether that noun is itself Spanish or English. In English, on the other hand, gender has lost its function as a grammatical category. Given the differences between the languages under consideration, we sought to establish how gender is assigned to nouns borrowed from a language in which gender is not an operative category into one in which it is.

The role played by speakers of different degrees of bilingual ability in gender assignment is still under debate. Haugen (1969) reports a large percentage of vacillation in assignment of gender to loanwords borrowed into Norwegian. Beardsmore (1971) claims that Belgian speakers "who do not keep their two languages separate" show deviant gender assignment patterns compared with the rest of the community. Barkin (1980) takes this tack further by correlating the lack of adaptation of a borrowed noun to Chicano Spanish patterns with the complete absence of gender indications on that noun.

We thus examined in the Puerto Rican community whether there is any weakening of this complex system of noun classification ascribable to the contact situation by comparing gender assignment patterns of the older and younger generations. We also sought to establish whether formal training in Spanish (i.e. participation in bilingual programs) is a differentiating factor in the children's behavior.

Accordingly, from the tape-recordings collected during the participant observation phase of the project, 474 instances of English nouns occurring in naturalistic Spanish discourse were extracted. These were coded according to whether or not gender was assigned as required by monolingual syntactic rules and if so, which one. Each noun was also coded for a number of factors which could conceivably contribute to the choice of masculine vs. feminine gender.

Because gender is a concord rule, its indications may be conveyed on determiners, adjectives or pronouns. As these are not always obligatory categories, and as gender distinctions are neutralized in some, there were many cases of borrowed nouns which did not show gender. In this connection, we examined for each borrowed noun whether or not a gender carrier was syntactically required. Examples where the carrier is not required in Spanish include mass nouns as in (1) plural nouns following verbs (2) and prepositions (3); gender distinctions are neutralized in unstressed possessives (3), etc.

1. Hasta ∅ *overtime* me dió. (01/3)[7] 'He even gave me overtime'.
2. Esos son ∅ *ups*. (01/3). 'Those are ups [uppers]'.
3. Le quitaron sus ∅ *estripes* y todo, y le pusieron en ∅ *plainclothes* a trabajar. (49/41) 'They took away his stripes and everything, and put him to work in plainclothes'.

Table 4 shows the proportion of gender expressed by children and adults according to syntactic requirements for its expression.

We first note that gender may be expressed, even when the determiner is not required or is uninflected for gender, via other sentence elements which are also gender carriers, as in example 4:

4. Yo creo que mi *hair* está lind*a*, beautiful. (2/334)
   'I think my hair is pretty, beautiful'.

TABLE 4 *Percentage of gender expressed according to syntactic requirement*

	Children	Adults
Gender Required	99% 172/173	99% 282/284
Gender not Required	4% 1/24	9% 11/118

However, when the expression of gender (or more accurately, expression of the gender carrier) is required in the recipient language, it is almost categorically expressed, by both children and adults, and regardless of whether the children had acquired Spanish formally, in bilingual education programs, or informally, in the community. These data, which include both phonologically integrated (e.g. *suera* 'sweater') and unintegrated (e.g. coat) borrowed nouns, confirm that the expression of gender does not depend on the degree of phonological integration of the borrowing, as Barkin (1980) claims, but on the syntactic rules of the recipient language. In fact, we found that children, some of whom have not yet completed the acquisition process, and who vary widely as to their bilingual ability, do not differ significantly from their parents in this regard. The complex system of noun classification, which is gender, appears to be internalized by children as early as age five, regardless of their formal training in Spanish.

Having ascertained that the use of the category of gender *per se* functions with borrowed nouns as in native ones, we next examined the factors which might determine the choice of masculine vs. feminine gender for a given noun, and isolated at least five. These are listed in Table 5; along with an example of the way the borrowed nouns in the corpus were coded.

Thus the occurrence of *shorty* was coded as M for physiological referent, since it referred to a male; *blackout* as Ø, since it has no animate referent, and so on.

Table 6 shows the proportion of feminine gender assigned to borrowed nouns by children and adults, as a function of each of the factors listed in Table 5.

As seen from Table 6, there is basically no difference between children and adults even in the subtle ranking of the factors contributing to the choice of gender. The one over-riding factor in determining gender choice is that of physiological sex when the referent is animate: neither children nor adults assign masculine gender to a noun referring to a female being or *vice versa*.[8]

Cases involving physiological sex, however, do not exceed more than about 10% of the total data base. The most important contribution to gender

TABLE 5 *Factors conditioning gender assignment*

Factor	Example	Code
Physiological sex of (animate) referent:	*shorty*	M
	cousin	F
	blackout	Ø
Phonological gender:	*suéter* 'sweater' (integrated)	M
	pencil (unintegrated)	M
	suera 'sweater' (integrated)	F
	orchestra (unintegrated)	F
	rai 'ride' (integrated)	Ø
	flowerseeds (unintegrated)	Ø
Analogical gender:	*building* (<el edificio)	M
	butterfly (<la mariposa)	F
	afro	Ø
Homophony:	*color* (<el color)	M
	jacket (<la chaqueta)	F
	coat	Ø
Suffixal analogy:	*language* (<el -aje)	M
	education (<la -ión)	F
	overtime	Ø

choice, when all the factors are considered simultaneously (though this does not emerge from Table 6; see Poplack, Pousada & Sankoff, 1982), is made by the phonological shape of the noun in question. The well-defined criteria depending on word-final segments by which gender is assigned to Spanish nouns also operate consistently to assign gender to borrowed nouns, even for those which show two alternative paths of phonological integration (*el suéter* ~ *la suera* 'sweater'; *el hambérguer* ~ *la hamberga* 'hamburger').

These results are illustrative of several points. Most notable is the finding that the "variations" or irregularities in gender assignment noted by scholars (e.g. Haugen, Beardsmore and Barkin) are practically non-existent in the Puerto Rican community, despite inclusion in the sample of speakers of varying bilingual abilities, and of children who have not yet completed acquiring either language as well as adults. The few cases of vacillation

TABLE 6 *Proportion of feminine gender assigned to borrowed nouns according to conditioning factors*

		All speakers		Adults		Children	
		F^a/N^b	%	F/N	%	F/N	%
Physiological gender:	M	0/29	0	0/13	0	0/16	0
	F	15/17	88	10/11	91	5/6	83
	Ø	46/428	11	21/269	8	25/159	16
Phonological gender:	M (int.)	8/130	6	8/94	8	0/36	0
	M (un.)	24/183	13	14/119	12	10/64	16
	F (int.)	10/12	83	3/5	60	7/7	100
	F (un.)	1/3	33	1/2	50	0/1	0
	Ø (int.)	4/21	19	0/11	0	4/10	40
	Ø (un.)	14/125	11	5/62	8	9/63	14
Analogical gender:	M	7/242	3	3/142	2	4/100	4
	F	46/158	29	24/92	26	22/66	33
	Ø	8/74	11	4/59	7	4/15	27
Homophony:	M	0/38	0	0/29	0	0/9	0
	F	7/22	32	5/16	31	2/6	33
	Ø	52/404	13	24/238	10	28/166	17
	either	2/10	20	2/10	20	0/0	
Suffixal analogy:	M	0/4	0	0/3	0	0/1	0
	F	1/9	11	1/8	13	0/1	0
	Ø	46/406	11	21/243	9	25/163	15
	TOTAL	61/474	13	31/293	11	30/181	17

[a]F = Feminine gender
[b]N = Total borrowed nouns

among recurring nouns were rarely on well-established borrowings. This, along with the findings presented in the previous section, confirms the strong role of the speech community in establishing norms for bilingual as well as monolingual linguistic behavior. This factor outweighs that of bilingual ability, since non-fluent bilinguals were found not to differ significantly from balanced bilinguals. In fact, it is evident that the criteria for gender assignment decisions have been largely internalized by children by the time they reach the first grade, and do not differ significantly thereafter, regardless of formal instruction in Spanish.

Indeed, we have demonstrated an overwhelming regularity in gender assignment among both children and adults by showing that well-defined criteria applying to native nouns also apply rigorously to borrowed material: words of English origin take on specific native grammatical functions. In virtually every case where the host language syntax requires the presence of a gender carrier, the borrowed noun is so accompanied, whether integrated into recipient language phonological and morphological patterns or not. Where assignment criteria depending on phonological segment are operative, these apply consistently, even for words which show two alternative paths of phonological integration. Thus it seems clear that nouns borrowed from English are subject to the same processes and constraints as the rest of the lexicon.

Code-switching

A final area of study concerns code-switching, or the alternation of two languages within a single discourse, sentence or constituent. This kind of discourse behavior, completely different from borrowing in nature, is generally frowned upon by teachers,[9] since, as one of them expressively put it,

Cuando uno mezcla dos idiomas, la sopa no sabe bien.
'When you mix two languages, the soup doesn't taste good'.

Large-scale quantitative studies of code-switching among the adults of this community — (Poplack, 1980, 1981; Sankoff & Poplack, 1981) have shown that code switching obeys a syntactic *Equivalence Constraint* — that is, switches occur at points in the sentence around which the order of sentence constituents must be grammatical with regard to both languages simultaneously. The over-whelming preference for switching at just such "equivalent" syntactic boundaries, rather than representing a deformation of linguistic skills, indicates a large degree of competence in both languages.

These constraints prevail, however, even in the discourse of non-fluent bilinguals. Since code-switching serves a variety of rhetorical and symbolic functions (e.g. Gumperz, 1976), these speakers have an interest in engaging in it despite their limited command of one of the codes. Indeed, it was found that the adults in the sample were able to participate in this verbal strategy regardless of bilingual ability by favoring one of three types of switches, each one characterized by switches of different levels of constituents, and each one reflecting different degrees of bilingual ability. We illustrate in following examples with data from their children, who were found to utilize the same types of switching:

5. *Tag-like Switch*:
   Oh, shit! Se fastidió todo el mundo aquí. (12/271) 'Everybody here got screwed.'
   Ay, pero don't hold on like that, man. (10/259). 'Hey, but . . .'
6. *Sentential Switch*:
   I don't know. *No habla como puertorriqueño*. (13/70). 'She doesn't speak like a Puerto Rican.'
   I wanna go swimming but it's too late. *¿Qué se puede hacer?* (15/150) 'What can you do?'
7. *Intra-sentential switch*:
   Y a la mamá le gustaba bailar *funky* (13/181). 'The mother liked to dance funky.'
   The baby fell *y se golpeó.* (15/102) '. . . and hurt himself.'

Example 5 shows a switch of an interjection, freely movable constituent which can be inserted almost anywhere in discourse, even with only minimal knowledge of L₂ (second language), without violating a grammatical rule of either language; example 6 shows a switch of a full sentence which, requires much more knowledge of L₂ to produce, but not as much as is required to switch within the confines of a single sentence (7). In order to produce this latter type of switch, the speaker must know enough about the grammar of each language and the way the two interact to avoid ungrammatical utterances.

In addition, the children displayed another type of code-switching behavior, which in fact accounts for 40% of all of their code-switches, in contrast to the adults, for whom it represented only a small proportion (under 10%): switching of a single noun. This is exemplified in example 8:

8. *"Single-noun" Switch*:
   Oh, boy! Let me get a *chicle!* (11/333) '. . . piece of gum'
   Get off my *d'eso* first. (15/150) '. . . whaddayacallit . . .'
   That ain't no *pichitito* (pichoncito), that's a owl! (03/005) '. . . pigeon . . .'

Figure 5 displays the strategy by which Spanish-dominant (or non-fluent) adult bilinguals (the broken line) are able to code-switch frequently, and still maintain grammaticality in both languages. The overwhelming majority of their switches are of tags, the type requiring least bilingual skill. The balanced bilingual adults, on the other hand, (the dotted line) favor the sentential or intrasentential type, which we had hypothesized to require most skill.[10] This allows non-fluent bilinguals to engage in interactions involving code-switching, without fear of violating the conditions on co-grammaticality which govern this discourse mode.

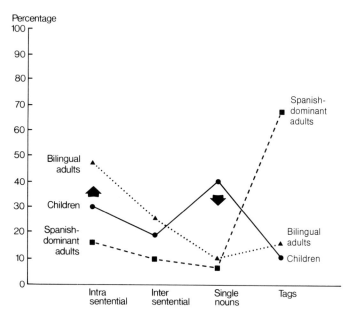

FIGURE 5 *Proportion of different code-switching types for adults and children.*

Examination of more than 600 code-switches occurring spontaneously in the tape-recorded speech of the children showed, surprisingly enough, considering the young age of some of them, that violations of the *Equivalence Constraint* were almost non-existent here as well. We do see from Figure 5, however, that the children form a group distinct from both balanced and non-fluent bilingual adults. For one thing, the striking pattern of tag use which characterizes the non-fluent bilingual adults is absent from the children. Whereas the use of tags is as low among children as among balanced bilingual adults, the children also use considerably less intra-sentential switches than those adults. On the other hand, they switch considerably more single nouns, as in example 8, than do any of the adults.

We believe this to be an acquisitional effect in two respects: 1) The degree of linguistic virtuosity required to engage in rapid intra-sentential switching is probably not yet fully developed among the children. 2) Their relatively early stage of vocabulary acquisition may account for a large proportion of the children's single-noun switches. Thus, in contrast to the use of tags among Spanish-dominant adults, this "single-noun switching" is *not* a strategy but in large part simply lack of lexical availability in one of the two languages, a situation which has been found not to hold for the adults in the community.

This ties in with McClure's (1981) findings that young bilingual Chicano children use more of what she calls "code-mixing", the inclusion of single items from one code into the discourse of another, while older children make greater use of "code-changing", which essentially involves the alternation of larger elements of discourse such as major constituents or sentences.

If the individual children represented in Figure 5 were separated out, we would find a transitional group to resemble the adults somewhat more, as indicated by the arrows in Figure 5, insofar as they use more intra-sentential and less single noun switches than their peers. This difference does not correlate with age, sex, or placement in a bilingual program. It may simply be that these children have better bilingual or verbal skills; we do not yet have enough data to judge.

Discussion

In conclusion, we summarize what the combination of ethnographic and sociolinguistic studies of children and their parents adds to our understanding of the evolution and maintenance of a stable bilingual community. The ethnographic observations have provided broad information about trends of language use, capable of supporting or disconfirming speakers' own reports of and attitudes toward the languages they speak, when and with whom.

In the Puerto Rican community of East Harlem, these observations have shown that the appropriate domains for use of English are expanding, but this is not accompanied by a concomitant decrease in use of Spanish. Rather, there is evidence that English and Spanish are used increasingly in conjunction among the younger generations. Thus outward appearance of language shift can, with some confidence, be interpreted in terms of language maintenance if one also takes into account the in-depth knowledge of the linguistic situation afforded by participant observation in the community.

The co-existence of Spanish and English without functional separation raises other questions of a purely linguistic nature, which observational methods alone are not equipped to handle: Are the two languages used sequentially or simultaneously? Is there "mixture" and how does it manifest itself? In borrowing? In code switching? What are the differential effects of either type of juxtaposition on the recipient language system?

To address these issues, we performed large-scale quantitative analyses of natural speech recorded as part of the ethnographic phase of the project. We focused on three aspects of the confrontation of Spanish and English observed to play a key role in the linguistic repertoires of the speakers: the mechanics of borrowing, the assignment of gender to loanwords and the use of code-switching. The results of these studies confirmed and deepened the findings of the ethnographic analysis.

Thus we saw that although the younger generations are responsible for introducing English into previously all-Spanish domains, the specific way they use English in no way represents a departure from the usage of their parents. On the contrary, the sociolinguistic analyses provide evidence of an overwhelming regularity in the introduction and incorporation of English loanwords into Spanish, a regularity which extends to the choice of morphophonological form in which the word is integrated. Contrary to previous hypotheses, children in this community do not assign English phonology and morphology to socially integrated loanwords, although they may possess sufficient knowledge of those patterns to do so. Rather, the word, along with its particular linguistic form, is transmitted across generations much the same way as monolingual neologisms. Similarly, study of the choice of which gender to assign to borrowed words shows that the factor that contributes most to the assignment of masculine or feminine gender is the phonological shape of the borrowed word, the same factor which basically explains gender assignment patterns to Spanish words. Here again, there is no variation to speak of between parents and children, just as there is virtually none in gender assignment to monolingual Spanish nouns.

These results, coupled with observations, provide a basis for stressing the strong role of the speech community in determining not only monolingual, but also bilingual, linguistic norms. We have already seen that this factor outweighs those of home language and school program in determining current language preference, especially for the boys. It is seen again in the establishment of community-wide rules for the incorporation of non-native linguistic material into the recipient language system.

In contrast to the striking similarities between adult and child behavior in the integration of loanwords into Spanish and their assignment to a gender, systematic sociolinguistic analysis reveals one area of bilingual grammar in which the younger generation diverges markedly from the older one: the use of code-switching. Whereas adults in the community, regardless of bilingual ability, use this discourse mode as an interactional strategy, such is not the case for the children. Although the latter, like their parents, displayed an overwhelming adherence to the syntactic co-grammaticality constraints on code-switching, they were seen to prefer switching one particular type of constituent, single nouns, in contrast to their parents. This suggests that much switching by children could be explained as a lack of lexical availability rather than a discourse strategy. This would make sense in view of the fact that children and pre-adolescents cannot be expected to have fully mastered the details of either the social interactional or the linguistic competence possessed by their elders.

The differential behaviour of the children with regard to loanword integration and gender assignment on the one hand, and code-switching on the other, also reflects the differential linguistic nature of these processes. Gender is an early acquisitional rule, acquired once and generalized thereafter. Loanwords are acquired on an individual basis, along with and in the same way as the rest of the lexicon. Code-switching, however, is a continuing maturational process similar to the development of stylistic and repertoire range. Code-switching of the intra-sentential type also requires full syntactic development of both languages, not yet the case of most of the children in the sample. This also ties in with the prevalence of single-noun switching found in the data.

The contribution of quantitative sociolinguistic analyses to the elaboration of our understanding of the intergenerational transmission of bilingual skills is clear. It should be equally clear that such analyses are meaningless if performed on data which are not contextually well-characterized or are of uncertain ethnographic pertinence.

The mutual validation of the ethnographic and variationist approaches, and the additional layer of explanation each provides for the other's results, leads to a fuller understanding of the intergenerational dynamics of language contact.

In closing one might ask what relevance these findings have for the maintenance of Spanish in the Puerto Rican community in New York.

In earlier studies the circulatory migration between Puerto Rico and New York was found to be an important factor in renewing the Spanish input into the bilingual situation. As for the children, it is clear that independent of whether they are in English classes (where no Spanish is taught), or in bilingual classes, those developments which have been shown to hold synchronically in adult speech are being effectively transmitted to the younger generations. In addition, the patterns of communication which are acquired early by these children, as well as their positive attitudes towards the learning and use of Spanish, combine with the demographic facts to ensure the perpetuation of bilingualism in the community.

Notes

1. This paper is a synthesis of some of the reports and publications issuing from the project: *Intergenerational Perspectives on Bilingualism: From Community to Classroom*, funded by the National Institute of Education, the Ford Foundation and The City University of New York. More details can be found in the fuller versions of the papers cited throughout this text. The ethnographic fieldwork from which the data are drawn was carried out among the adults in the community by Pedro Pedraza and among the children by Alicia Pousada and Pedro Pedraza. This paper was first presented at the Language Proficiency Assessment Symposium in March 1981, and has since benefited from the critical comments of colleagues at the Center for Puerto Rican Studies.

2. This designation of "both", in most instances, refers to use of Spanish and English with the same interlocutor. However it should be noted that there are also cases which do not emerge from this treatment of the data where language choice varies according to the interlocutor: e.g. children frequently address younger siblings in Spanish, and older or same-age siblings in English or both. Likewise, in bilingual classrooms, there are children of varying abilities in Spanish and English, who are often addressed according to their preference.

3. The analysis reported in this section, based on the ethnographic field work of Pousada and Pedraza, has grown out of close collaboration with them.

4. E.g. older, Spanish-dominant or monolingual speakers, married women and young children are normally addressed in Spanish (see Pedraza, 1981).

5. This configuration basically characterizes the sample of adults and children under consideration here.

6. It is of course also possible that this is an acquisitional effect. As the children acquire greater experience in both Spanish and English their scores may reach the level of their parents.

7. Numbers in parentheses refer to speaker and example codes.

8. The two exceptions we found are *un lesbian* which is phonologically masculine, and *un cow*, which may not have been perceived as being feminine by the child who uttered it.

9. Pousada reports that most of the teachers of these children do not raise serious objections to their switching in the classroom, although the teachers do report that they usually supply a monolingual version of the code-switched utterance.

10. The lines on the graph represent an average over all speaker, but most of the individuals in the group show the same distinctive pattern.

References

Barkin, F. 1980, The role of loanword assimilation in gender assignment. *The Bilingual Review.*

Beardsmore, H. 1971, A gender problem in a language contact situation. *Lingua*, 27, 141–59.

Cornejo, R. 1973, The acquisition of lexicon in the speech of bilingual children. In P. Turner (ed.), *Bilingualism in the Southwest.* Tucson: University of Arizona Press.

Fishman, J. 1966, *Language loyalty in the United States.* The Hague: Mouton.

Fries, C. & Pike, K. 1949, Coexistent phonemic systems. *Language*, 25, 29–50.

Gal, S. 1978, Variation and change in patterns of speaking: Language shift in Austria. In D. Sankoff (ed.), *Linguistic variation: Models and methods.* New York: Academic Press.

Gumperz, J. 1972, Introduction. In J. Gumperz & D. Hymes (eds), *Directions in sociolinguistics.* New York: Holt, Rinehart and Winston, Inc.

— 1976, The sociolinguistic significance of conversational code-switching. *Working papers of the Language Behavior Research Laboratory #46.* Berkeley: University of California.

Harris, T. 1979, *The prognosis for Judeo-Spanish: Its description, survival and decline, with implications for the study of language death in general.* Unpublished doctoral dissertation, Georgetown University.

Haugen, E. 1950, The analysis of linguistic borrowing. *Language*, 26, 210–31.

— 1956, Bilingualism in the Americas: A bibliography and research guide. *American Dialect Society Monograph*, 26.

— 1969, *The Norwegian language in America.* Philadelphia: University of Pennsylvania Press.

Labov, W. 1966, *The social stratification of English in New York City.* Washington, D.C.: Center for Applied Linguistics.

— 1972, *Language in the inner city.* Philadelphia: University of Pennsylvania Press.

Labov, W., Cohen, P., Robins, C. and Lewis, J. 1968, *A study of the non-standard English of Negro and Puerto Rican speakers in New York City* (Report on Cooperative Research Project #3288). New York: Columbia University.

Language Policy Task Force, 1980, Social dimensions of language use in East Harlem. *Working Paper #7.* New York: Center for Puerto Rican Studies.

McClure, E. 1981, Formal and functional aspects of the code-switched discourse of bilingual children. In R. Duran (ed.), *Latino discourse and communicative behavior.* Norwood, N. J.: Ablex Publishing Corp.

Pedraza, P. 1981, *Ethnographic observations of language use in El Barrio.* Unpublished manuscript.

Poplack, S. 1980, "Sometimes I'll start a sentence in Spanish Y TERMINO EN ESPANOL": Toward a typology of code-switching. *Linguistics*, 18, 581–618.

— 1981, Syntactic structure and social function of code-switching. In R. Duran (ed.), *Latino discourse and communicative behavior*, Norwood, N. J.: Ablex Publishing Corp.

— 1982, Bilingualism and the vernacular. In B. Hartford, A. Valdman and C. Foster (eds) *Issues in international bilingual education: The role of the vernacular.* Plenum Publishing Co.

Poplack, S., Pousada, A. & Sankoff, D. 1982, Competing influences on gender assignment: Variable process, stable outcome. *Lingua*, 56, 139–66.

Poplack, S. & Sankoff, D. 1980, *Borrowing: The synchrony of integration*. Paper presented at the Linguistic Society of America (LSA) annual meeting, San Antonio, Texas

Sankoff, D. & Poplack, S. 1981, A formal grammar for code-switching. *Papers in Linguistics*, 14(1), 3–46.

Varo, C. 1971, *Consideraciones antropológicas y políticas en torno a la enseñanza del "Spanglish" en Nueva York*. Río Piedras: Ediciones Librería Internacional.

Studying Puerto Rican children's informal education at home

Evelyn Jacob
George Mason University, Fairfax, UA and
Centre for Applied Linguistics, Washington, D.C.

Many minority children in the United States experience problems in formal school settings; Puerto Rican students are no exception. One hypothesis used to explain these problems is that there is a "mismatch" between the social interaction rules and the informal education minority children experience in their homes and the social interaction rules and educational processes found in the schools (Philips, 1972). Some recent research (Lein, 1975; Philips, 1972; Jordan, 1977) has documented this mismatch between minority children's social interaction styles at home and those used in school. Unfortunately, very little is known about the informal educational experiences of Puerto Rican children or other children in Western, industrialized societies.

The research discussed here addresses this gap in the research literature. It utilizes previously collected, naturalistic observations to describe and analyze Puerto Rican children's informal skill education at home.[1] Because there are few detailed analyses of naturally occurring informal education among children, the approach and procedures developed are stressed rather than conclusions. Results of a sample of data — girls' literacy activities — are also presented in this report.

Previous research and present goals

Available literature on informal education reveals three different foci in defining this notion: topic, method and setting. Cohen (1971, pp. 25, 36) stresses topic and method in his definition of informal education as "the inculcation of basic psychological patterns through spontaneous interaction with parents, siblings, and others". He contrasts this to formal education which is "the inculcation of standardized knowledge and skills by standardized and stereotyped means". Scribner & Cole (1973, pp. 554–5) define informal education on the basis of setting and method as that which "occurs in the course of mundane adult activities in which the young take part according to their abilities". Childs & Greenfield (1980, p. 269) define it in terms of setting, as that "occurring in situations that are part of everyday life rather than specifically set up for educational purposes". Although these definitions differ somewhat in focus, they are similar in that they seek to identify a kind of education that does not occur in formal, school-type environments.[2]

Anthropologists have provided descriptions of informal education in non-school settings from many traditional, non-industrialized societies (e.g. Fortes, 1938; Mead, 1928; Middleton, 1970; O'Neale, 1932; Whiting, 1941). In their reviews of these studies, Childs & Greenfield (1980) and Scribner & Cole (1973) summarize certain generalizations about informal education: learning occurs in contexts where the significance of what is to be learned is intrinsic in the context; learning is primarily observational; participatory learning also is an important method; there is little verbal formulation on the part of the learner; learners rarely ask questions; there is a negative relationship between "why" questions and the degree to which the learner participates in the activity to be learned; and the personal nature of the relationship between the learner and the teacher is an important motivational factor.

These generalizations about informal education in traditional non-industrialized societies contrast with many features of education in formal school settings in our society. However, in order to examine the "mismatch" hypothesis it must be determined whether informal education experienced by minority children in our society is similar to that described above. If, in fact, these generalizations are true for the informal education of minority groups within our society, then, as Scribner & Cole (1973, p. 558) point out, "It is not necessary to look further for explanation of the difficulties formal education may present to people who rely heavily on informal education as their basic method".

The next question to consider is what information exists about the informal education of minority group children in our society. The answer is that very little naturalistic data currently are available.[3] The most complete naturalistic data exist for American Indian groups. Philips (1972, p. 387) outlines an idealized learning sequence based on her observations of Warm Springs Indians: "(1) observation which, of course, includes listening; (2) supervised participation; and (3) private, self-initiated self-testing". This sequence and her description are consistent with the generalizations offered from research in traditional societies (see also Cazden & John, 1971). But Philips' work also indicates that there may be a variety of types of learning activities and events that occur in children's lives. After presenting the idealized learning sequence quoted above she adds:

"It is not the case that all acquisition of skills proceed through such phases, however, but rather only some of these skills that Indian adults consciously and deliberately teach their children, and which the children consciously try to learn" (p. 387).

Unfortunately, there are no detailed descriptions of the educational activities and events occurring in Puerto Rican homes on the mainland or the island. In reviewing the previous research little naturalistic evidence could be found. Steward *et al.* (1956, pp. 145; 220) mention that imitative play was observed in the central and western regions of the island. In a more recent study of life in a poor urban shanty town in San Juan, Safa (1974, p. 54) reports that children's play is often based on imitations of adult life. These few comments fail to provide a useful picture of the education that occurs in Puerto Rican homes today.

The goals of this study are to provide a description of the variety of methods used in the education of Puerto Rican children at home, to examine variability among groups of children, and to test whether the generalizations about informal education developed from research in traditional societies are valid for this sample. To meet these goals topic and setting have been used to delimit the scope of the study; method is allowed to vary. The teaching and learning of skills (as opposed to cultural values and language) in the home setting is the focus. Within the category of skills three have been chosen for detailed analysis: literacy, chores and rule-bound games. These were chosen because behaviors related to them occur relatively frequently in the observations, they provide a diverse sample of kinds of skills to be learned, and they differ in their functional significance in the culture. Literacy is related to school performance, chores are related to adult roles, and rule-bound games are important in the children's world of play.

Data base

The present study is based on data that were collected during 1974–75 in the town of Utuado, Puerto Rico, as part of a larger study of the relationships among culture, environment and cognition. The goals of the previous study were to produce an ethnography of children in the town; to do a quantitative analysis of the relationships among culture, environment, and cognition; and to collect a data base on a random sample of children for use in future analyses (see Jacob, 1977, for details). These data include detailed and naturalistic observations of the children's activities at home and in school, interviews with their teachers and female caretakers, their scores on cognitive tests, and their school record data. The detailed observations of the children in the sample at home are the focus of the analysis in this paper. There were 29 children in the sample: 14 were middle-class and 15 lower-class; 17 were male and 12 were female. The mean age of the children was 6 years-3 months at the time of data collection. All attended kindergarten during the 1974–75 school year.

Observations in the home were conducted by the author and four Puerto Rican research assistants between 9 a.m. and 6 p.m., during the children's summer vacation between kindergarten and first grade. Four home observations were done for each child; two were approximately 15 minutes long and two were about 30 minutes long. Only one observer was present during each observation.

Observers were instructed not to interact with the child or others present during the observation. They were to try to maintain "the role of a friendly, non-evaluating, non-directive and non-participating person who is interested in what people do" (Barker & Wright, 1971, p. 211). The observers sat near the child they were to observe and placed a small tape recorder with a built-in microphone near him/her. Before beginning the observation, the observers waited a few minutes after their arrival to allow for an adjustment period. During the observations no constraints were placed on the children; they were free to go anywhere or do anything they wanted. The observers made notes of what the child did and said, and what others said to the child and did. In particular, they were instructed to note what the child did, how she or he did it, with whom, what objects or toys were used, and the interactions between child and others. They were also instructed to note, when possible, the actions and speech of those with whom the child interacted and of those near the child. It was stressed that they were to provide *descriptions* and not evaluations of the children's activities.

After doing the assigned observation, the observers expanded the notes and transcribed the tape made during the observation. They then integrated their expanded description with the transcription of the audio tape in the form of a continuous narrative. The narratives were then checked, revised and typed.

Issues in studying informal education in naturalistic settings

Using the methods outlined above, samples were collected from the children's "stream of behavior" (see Barker, 1963). These data provide information on the participants' attitudes and values about education as well as their educational activities and environments. Because the analyses to date have focused on the participants' educational activities and environments, these topics are the foci of the rest of the paper. In approaching the data, several issues became apparent.

The first involves the conceptualization and identification of informal education. Education includes both teaching and learning, and any discussion must deal with both parts of the process. Teaching does not appear hard to identify. Gumperz & Herasimchuk (1975) have defined it as a situation in which two or more people focus on a particular task, and one person assumes and is accorded the role of "expert" relative to one or more other participants. Following this definition, most would agree that the following situation involves teaching: A five-year-old and his mother are seated next to one another on the floor in the living room of their home. Plastic numbers are scattered in front of them. The mother picks up the plastic number one, holds it up in front of the child and says "one", prompting the child to repeat what she said. After the child says the number, the mother picks up the plastic two, and repeats the process through the number nine.

The issue of identifying learning, on the other hand, presents certain problems. Stevenson (1972, p. 2) points to one: "Everyone would agree that learning involves a change in behavior as a result of experience. But learning itself can never be observed. We must make inferences about learning from changes in performance". In naturalistic settings this is particularly problematic because the change in behavior may be manifested a long time after the event that triggered it. To compound the problem, even when a change in behavior is observed one cannot be sure if the change was a result of learning or some other event.

The difficulties encountered in identifying learning in naturalistic settings resulted in a focus on describing "teaching and learning environments" rather than describing "teaching and learning". Learning environment refers to those social and physical settings which provide children with opportunities to learn specific topics or skills. Moore (1980) presents a similar orientation. He states, "We have been taking as problematic the process by which participants in a specific social environment organize their interactions in such a way as to make learning possible".

The home environment provides a variety of opportunities for teaching and learning of skills. Some of these can be considered implicit learning opportunities and other present more explicit opportunities for children's learning. For example, books present in the home and adult literacy activities which take place there offer implicit literacy learning opportunities for children. They provide a background which may then be transformed by the child or others into explicit learning opportunities.[4] Casual observation of these artifacts and their uses may enable children to develop some attitudes about the importance of particular types of literacy artifacts and activities. However, they must more explicitly observe, participate or be taught in order for them to learn literacy skills.

Another problem was the development of a unit of analysis for the explicit learning opportunities. After studying the data, the notion of "potential learning activity" (PLA) was developed. By this is meant a behavior or sequence of behaviors that can result in learning on a specified topic. (It is important to add the qualification "on a specified topic" because *any* activity is a potential learning activity with regard to *some* topic.) The target child doing an activity related to the topic, explicitly watching others doing such an activity, or receiving verbal instructions on the topic were activities that triggered identification of a PLA.

Procedure

Four preliminary steps were developed for the analysis of informal education in the narrative observations: indexing, identifying PLAs, bracketing PLAs, and coding the PLAs on a variety of variables. These steps, performed separately for each of the three topics (literacy, chores, rule-bound games), are:

1. *Indexing.* In order to be able to identify both the implicit and explicit learning opportunities (as well as the attitudes and values expressed about the particular topic) everyone's behavior related to a given topic as well as all references made in conversation to the topic were indexed on coding sheets.

2. *Identifying PLAs.* The coders then identified the target children's PLAs from all the behaviors indexed. The target child engaging in an activity related to the specified topic, explicitly watching others doing such an activity, or receiving verbal instructions on the topic are activities that marked initial identification of a PLA.

3. *Bracketing PLAs.* Once the PLAs were identified, the coders

worked both forward and backward from the identifying activity to bracket the beginning and end of the PLA. A variety of contextualization cues (see Dickman, 1963; Erickson & Shultz, 1981) were used for this: linguistic signals that label an activity or summon the child's participation, change in gross physical movement of the target child, change in topic of conversation, change in artifacts the target child uses, and change in the behavior of the person observed.

4. *Coding of PLAs.* The PLAs were coded for type, topic, length, initiator, and participants involved other than the target child. If the target child observed someone, who it was and what they were doing were also coded. The presence of direct instruction during the PLA was noted.

The procedures outlined here resulted in the identification and preliminary analysis of the explicit learning opportunities of the target children.

Literacy education environments for girls

For indexing and bracketing the observations a very broad definition of literacy was used and included reading,[5] writing, counting, watching television and preliteracy activities such as coloring and doing puzzles. Anderson, Teale & Estrada (1980) followed a similar approach in their study of the literacy environments and activities of children from low income families.

The observations were examined for the girls' implicit literacy education environments. An inventory of the literacy artifacts present in the homes and mentioned in the observations revealed that televisions, *libretas* (school notebooks), and writing implements were present in most homes. Books, radios or record players and clocks or watches were present in over a third of the homes. A variety of other artifacts were present less frequently.[6]

Female caretakers of the girls had been asked how many and what kinds of books were in their homes. The responses to the quantitative question ranged between 0 and 300, with a median of 6 and a mean of 58. Five of the caretakers listed the types of books that were in their homes. *Novelas* (novels), dictionaries, sport books and encyclopedias were each mentioned in two households. Types of books mentioned once are magazines, newspapers, the Bible, classical novels, story books and books about biology, history or religion.

The girls' environment beyond their homes has many examples of literacy materials. These are signs on the streets and in shop windows; newspapers are sold on street corners; and most goods and products sold have labels or directions on them.

On examining the girls' potential learning activities four types of PLAs were identified which are ranked here from the most frequent to the least frequent in the sample: (1) child engages in a literacy activity alone; (2) child engages in a literacy activity with another; (3) child imitates another's literacy activity; and (4) child observes another's literacy activity.[7] Examples of each of these types of PLAs are presented below. These findings do not support the generalization from the cross-cultural literature that observation is a primary method of informal education. However, they do support the generalization that participatory learning is important.

The following episode provides an example of a girl doing a literacy activity alone. In this case, her counting identified the PLA.

Example 1[8]

Raquel (the target child) is alone in a bedroom in her grandparents' home. She has been looking through a box, removing objects from it and putting them on the arm of a nearby chair:

Raquel comes to a piece of paper.
Raquel opens the piece of paper, saying, " . . . the picture I made".
Raquel says to herself, " . . . flowers — they need — one, two, three — four, five, six, seven — they need seven."

Raquel then returns to the living room where she talks with her grandmother.

In Example 2 the target girl and her mother jointly perform the task of reading syllables in the child's school notebook.

Example 2

Maria (the target child), her siblings and her mother are at home. The observation starts with Maria standing near the kitchen counter watching her mother sharpen a pencil with a knife; she seems anxious for her mother to finish. The other children are in the living room; Maria's seven-year-old sister (Carmen) is kneeling on the floor, writing in a school notebook; at one point she sings to herself as she writes, "I'm going to study today, everything, everything, I'm studying, I'm going to study". The PLA begins:

Maria returns to living room from kitchen.
Maria sits in chair.

Maria (looks at her school notebook and reads outloud): "Bo, bu, bu."
Carmen watches Maria read.
Maria: "Co."
Carmen (to Maria): "No, it isn't 'bu', here it says 'co'."
Maria gets up from her chair and runs to the kitchen.
Maria (to mother): "Mom, does it say 'co'?"
Mother (to Maria): "Ca."
Maria returns to her chair and looks at an open page in her notebook.
Maria (calls to her mother): "Mom, I forgot."
Mother walks to Maria's chair from the kitchen.
Mother (to Maria): "I'm not going to come in here every minute telling
   you what it is, understand. Show me where you are", as she takes the
   notebook.
Mother (points to the book and says to Maria): "Let's see, what is this
   one?"
Maria (to mother): "Move your finger — bu."
Mother (to Maria): "Bo — say 'bo' . . . and the other one below."
Maria (to mother): " . . ."
Mother (to Maria): "Ca."
Maria (to mother): "Ba."
Mother (to Maria): "Which?"
Maria (to mother): "Ba", pointing to syllable in book.
Mother (to Maria): "Ca!"
Maria (to mother): "Oh, ca."

The PLA continues for approximately another 20 minutes. Maria and her
mother continue reading the syllables for another 2 minutes then Maria says,
"Now I've studied that". Carmen tells her sister to write her name, and
Maria's mother repeats the direction. With help from her mother and sister,
Maria copies her name into the notebook.

The next example shows a girl imitating another's apparent counting
activity.

Example 3
   Luz Maria (the target child) and her sister Claribel (8 years old) are in
the living room. Luz Maria has been removing plastic fruit from a bowl and
carefully setting them in a row along the back of the sofa; her sister is
watching her as she does this. Then:

   Luz Maria sits on the edge of the sofa.
   Claribel continues to sit on the far right edge of the sofa away from the
   fruit and watches Luz Maria.

Claribel touches each fruit slowly, starting with the farthest piece (as if counting them although nothing is said aloud).
Luz Maria watches Claribel.
Luz Maria pushes herself to the back of the sofa.
Luz Maria jumps off the sofa and turns around to face the fruit.
Luz Maria touches all the fruit slowly, starting with the fruit on the far left (as if counting them).

Their mother walks into the living room and tells Luz Maria to take the fruit bowl off the sofa so it doesn't fall off and break. Luz Maria takes the bowl off the sofa and puts it and the fruit along the bottom of the wall.

In the following example, the target girl observes her sister writing as they prepare to pretend play.

Example 4
Luz (the target child), her sister Sandra (12 years old), and Luz's friend Zulmarie (6 years old) are in Luz's living room. They have been getting ready to pretend that they are going shopping. Luz and Sandra have brought a pile of things (a brush, lipstick, plastic case, pencil and notebook) to the record player. Luz says, "And this was my store", and Sandra agrees. When another sister arrives in the house Luz asks her to look for their play money. Before it is found she says she wants to start. Luz and Sandra begin playing; Sandra pretends to sell Luz some of the items and Luz pretends to pay for them. Sandra then begins to write in a notebook to make pretend money:

Sandra writes in school notebook.
Luz looks at what Sandra is writing.
Luz (to Sandra): "Hurry up . . . I have to go shopping."
Sandra continues to write in the notebook
Luz continues to watch what Sandra is writing.

After this PLA, Sandra and Luz change the game and play doctors, pretending that the pieces of paper are prescriptions instead of money.

PLAs in which the target child is reading or writing alone or with another were selected for further examination. The results are summarized here.

The first question asked was the nature of the content of the reading and writing activities the children did. When reading alone the girls usually looked at a book, *libreta*, (school notebook), or pamphlet without talking aloud during the process. Reading with another usually involved reading syllables or words aloud from a *libreta*; in one case it involved a newspaper.

Writing alone involved copying syllables or words in the *libreta*. Writing with another involved the target child writing words or her name with the help of another.

Most of the girls' reading and writing PLAs involved *libretas*. These are small notebooks that each child has in kindergarten. During the school year the children write syllables, words, numbers and their names in *libretas*; they also use them to practise reading. The significant role that this *school* literacy artifact has in the children's *home* literacy activities raises an important point. Most of the focus recently has been on home influences on school behavior. This finding points to the reciprocal nature of the influences, and suggests that, for these children, literacy may be defined primarily as a "school" activity (see Miller, 1981b, for similar results).

The second question was who initiated the PLAs. The solitary PLAs were all initiated by the target child herself. Most of the PLAs that involved the child and others were either initiated by the child herself or she initiated her participation in the activity. An example of this last category occurred when a girl's grandmother and older brother were reading syllables from a school notebook. The target child approached them, watched them, and then began to respond to the grandmother's questions; she had not initiated the PLA but had initiated her participation in it.

The finding that the girls themselves initiated their participation in the PLAs is consistent with the Puerto Rican notion of *capacidad*. Ethnographic work in the town had identified this concept which could be translated as capacity or ability. However, it has a much fuller connotation of a person's present abilities, social maturity and readiness to learn more complex skills or social behavior. The children's mothers felt that *capacidad* is increased little by little through the accumulation of experience. Young children are said to have no *capacidad*; as they gain experience (*coge experiencia*) they increase their *capacidad*. Several mothers said that since children learn little by little, one should not demand a lot of the children (*no exigirles mucho*). This concept would lead us to expect that adults and older siblings might wait for expressions of interest on the child's part before trying to teach them certain skills. This is supported by the data on girls' literacy learning.

The only functions of reading and writing that the girls participated in themselves during these PLAs were studying (including practising) and solitary reading. However, this does not mean that the girls were not aware of other functions of literacy. Some of the girls' behaviors that involved *pretend* reading and writing indicated their awareness of other literacy functions. For example, in one case, a girl and her older brother pretended that the back of a chair was a shopping list while playing with Barbie dolls. In another case, pages of a daily calendar were torn off and used as "pretend" food stamps. These activities were not included as PLAs because they did not seem to present explicit opportunities to learn the *skills* of reading, writing, or counting. They do, however, represent an important area where the girls seem to be learning about the *functions* of literacy. For the sample of girls' literacy activities discussed here, learning the skills and the functions of literacy are not coterminus. This does not support the generalization from cross-cultural literature that in informal education the significance of the skill to the learner is intrinsic in the context of learning. More "real world" uses of literacy were observed in the girls' pretending activities than in their potential learning activities.

Summary

This paper has focused on the procedures developed for identifying and analyzing the learning environments of Puerto Rican children from stream of behavior data using the notion of potential learning activity. A preliminary analysis of Puerto Rican girls' literacy education environments has also been presented. Interview and observation findings indicate that literacy materials are a part of the girls' homes lives, and that the number and nature of the artifacts vary across homes. It was found that most of the girls' potential literacy learning activities were self-initiated and that this is consistent with the Puerto Rican concept of *capacidad*. Literacy artifacts from school play an important part in the girls' home literacy activities, which suggests that literacy might be defined as a "school" activity by these children. Engaging in reading and writing either alone or with another were the most frequent type of potential learning activities, and observation of others' literacy activities was the least frequent. Only two functions of reading and writing (studying and solitary reading) were evident in the PLAs while others were exhibited in *pretend* reading and writing activities.

These findings provide an insight into the nature of the home literacy education environment in Puerto Rico and do not support some of the cross-cultural generalizations from research in traditional, non-industrialized societies. Any discussions of mismatch between children's home and school learning environments must be based on data from the two settings being compared and not on their assumed characteristics.

Notes

1. The author would like to thank Robert Russell, Roger Shuy and Walt Wolfram for comments on an earlier draft of this paper. The careful and reflective

approach to data coding exhibited by Joanne Bisagna, Emma Muñoz Duston
and Ramonita Santiago was important in the refinement of the procedures
outlined here. Support for this analysis was provided by the National Institute of
Education Grant NIE-G-80-0132. Data collection in Puerto Rico was supported
by the National Science Foundation, the Social Science Research Council, and
the American Association of the University of Women.
These data were collected on the island of Puerto Rico. Because of the high
degree of movement and migration between the island and the mainland, the
results of this analysis are expected to be relevant to both mainland and island
school.

2. Greenfield & Lave (1981) have pointed out that it is more appropriate to see
   informal education and formal education as extremes of a continuum rather than
   as a dichotomy. A paper by Catherine Cooper (*Children's discourse in
   cooperative and didactic interaction: Developmental patterns in effective learning*,
   presented at the National Institute of Education Mid-Project Research Forum
   Conference: Teaching as a Linguistic Process, in Fredericksburg, Virginia, in
   1979) and a recent study by LeCompte (1978) have implicitly defined informal
   education in terms of method and examined informal education occurring in
   formal school settings.

3. Evidence from mother-child interactions in laboratory settings is not applicable
   here because of the inappropriateness of generalizing from behavior in these
   settings to home settings (e.g. Belsky, 1979, 1980). There is a large body of work
   on children's language acquisition, some of which deals with the nature of the
   educational process. For example, Miller (1981a) describes mothers' direct
   instruction of language to their two-year old daughters. However, because the
   focus here is on *skill* education and not language learning we will not deal with
   this literature.

4. Anderson (1980) makes a similar point about the relationship between
   literacy materials and literacy activities: " . . . The mere presence of literacy
   materials is not necessarily indicative of the degree of a literacy environment.
   Materials must always be examined vis-à-vis the activities which are occurring."

5. We have treated looking at printed materials as "reading" for our purposes here.

6. All observations were examined and literacy artifacts present in the homes and
   mentioned in the observations were listed. Because the focus of the earlier data
   collection was not literacy, we had not made a systematic effort to record literacy
   artifacts. Consequently, these data do not provide a complete inventory of all
   literacy artifacts present in the homes, but they do provide some comparative
   data. Because of the procedures followed in recording the observations, literacy
   artifacts actually used by the target child and others present in the home are
   more likely to be recorded than artifacts merely present.

7. PLAs which involve the target child watching television or observing the
   researcher write are not included here.

8. The PLAs in each example are preceded and followed by summaries of the
   surrounding activities. The PLAs themselves are indented and taken directly
   from the observations. Some PLAs have been edited slightly to remove others'
   activities that appear extraneous to the PLA of interest. The dialogue was
   conducted in Spanish; the author did the translations. Dashes (--) indicate a
   pause; dots (. . .) indicate unintelligible words or phrases. Brackets indicate
   simultaneous activities.

References

Anderson, A. B. *Literacy resources: How preschoolers interact with written communication* (Quarterly report). Washington, D.C.: National Institute of Education, July 1980.

Anderson, A. B., Teale, W. H. & Estrada, E. 1980, Low-income children's preschool literacy experiences: Some naturalistic observations. *Quarterly Newsletter of the Laboratory of Comparative Human Cognition*, 2, 59–65.

Barker, R. 1963, The stream of behavior as an empirical problem. In R. Barker (ed.), *The stream of behavior*. New York: Appleton-Century-Crofts.

Barker, R. G. & Wright, H. F. 1971, *Midwest and its children*. Hamden, Connecticut: Archon Books (Originally published, Evanston, Illinois: Row, Peterson, 1955.)

Belsky, J. 1979, The effects of context on mother-child interaction: A complex issue. *Quarterly Newsletter of the Laboratory of Comparative Human Congition*, 1, 29–31.

— 1980, Mother-infant interaction at home and in the laboratory: A comparative study. *Journal of Genetic Psychology*, 137, 37–47.

Cazden, C. & John, V. 1971, Learning in American Indian children. In M. Wax, S. Diamond & F. O. Gearing (eds), *Anthropological perspectives on education*. New York: Academic Press.

Childs, C. P. & Greenfield, P. M. 1980, Informal modes of learning and teaching: The case of Zinacanteco weaving. In N. Warren (ed.), *Advances in cross-cultural psychology* (Vol. 2). London: Academic Press.

Cohen, Y. 1971, The shaping of men's minds: Adaptations to the imperatives of culture. In M. Wax, S. Diamond & F. O. Gearing (eds), *Anthropological perspectives on education*. New York: Basic Books.

Dickman, H. R. 1963, The perception of behavior units. In R. Barker (ed.), *The stream of behavior*. New York: Appleton-Century-Crofts.

Erickson, F. & Shultz, J. 1981, In J. Green & C. Wallat (eds), *Ethnography and language in educational settings*. Norwood, New Jersey: Ablex.

Fortes, M. 1938, Social and psychological aspects of education in Taleland. *Africa*, 11, 4.

Greenfield, P. M. & Lave, J. 1981, Cognitive aspects of informal education. In D. Wagner & H. Stevenson (eds), *Cultural perspectives on child development*. San Francisco: Freeman.

Gumperz, J. & Herasimchuk, E. 1975, The conversational analysis of social meaning: A study of classroom interaction. In M. Sanches & B. Blount (eds), *Sociocultural dimensions of language use*. New York: Academic Press.

Jacob, E. 1977, *The influence of culture and environment on cognition: A case study in a Puerto Rican town*. Unpublished doctoral dissertation, University of Pennsylvania.

Jordan, C. 1977, *Maternal teaching, peer teaching and school adaptation in an urban Hawaiian population*. Paper presented at the Society for Cross-Cultural Research Meetings, East Lansing, Michigan, February.

LeCompte, M. 1978, Learning to work: The hidden curriculum of the classroom. *Anthropology and Education Quarterly*, 9, 22–37.

Lein, L. 1975, You were talkin' though, Oh yes, you was. *Council on Anthropology and Education Newsletter*, 6, 1–11.

Mead, M. 1928, *Coming of age in Samoa*. New York: Morrow.

Middleton, J. 1970, *From child to adult: Studies in the anthropology of education*. Garden City, New York: The Natural History Press.

Miller, P. J. 1981a, *Amy, Wendy, and Beth: Learning language in south Baltimore*. Austin: University of Texas Press.

— 1981b, *Early socialization for schooling in a working-class community*. Paper presented at the University of Pennsylvania Ethnography in Education Research Forum, Philadelphia.

Moore, D. 1980, *Discovering the pedagogy of experience*. Paper presented at the American Anthropological Association meetings, Washington, D.C.

O'Neale, L. M. 1932, Yurok-Karok basket weavers. *University of California Publications in American Archeology and Ethnology*, 32, 10–11.

Philips, S. U. 1972, Participant structures and communicative competence: Warm Springs children in community and classroom. In C. Cazden, V. John, & D. Hymes (eds), *Functions of language in the classroom*. New York: Teachers College Press.

Safa, H. I. 1974, *The urban poor of Puerto Rico: A study in development and inequality*. New York: Holt, Rinehart, and Winston.

Scribner, S. & Cole, M. 1973, Cognitive consequences of formal and informal education, *Science*, 182, 553–9.

Stevenson, H. 1972, *Children's learning*. New York: Appleton-Century-Crofts.

Steward, J., *et al.* 1956, *The people of Puerto Rico*. Urbana: University of Illinois Press.

Whiting, J. W. M. 1941, *Becoming a Kwoma*. New Haven: Yale University Press.

PART II

New forms of assessment: The Tucson projects

An ethnographic approach to bilingual language proficiency assessment

Susan U. Philips
University of Arizona,
Tucson, Arizona

Bilingual education programs in the United States are primarily the result of the recognition of the right to an equal education for language minority students through such legislation as the *Bilingual Education Act of 1968* and the *Civil Rights Act of 1964.* Children whose first language is not English (and these are overwhelmingly Spanish in language background) generally have had lower scores on school achievement tests than monolingual English speakers. It has been argued that bilingual education would provide bilingual children with equal access to the educational system and eradicate the achievement score disparities between bilingual and monolingual children.

In fact, such eradication of achievement score disparities has not occurred. Because some educators believe that poor assessment procedures are contributing to the continued difficulty school systems are having in raising the achievement scores of bilingual students, increased attention is now being given to bilingual language proficiency assessment practices.

An ethnographic approach to language proficiency assessment of language minority children stresses the need to develop assessment procedures within a general framework that assumes culture-specific developmental sequences in the acquisition of communicative competence. It is necessary to determine empirically what those sequences are before teachers and curriculum developers can build on already existing cognitive development in their education of the children. For this reason, bilingual language proficiency assessment in all settings should entail not just evaluation of students' language skills in terms of an already known and established set of criteria, but it should also include *RESEARCH,* open-ended exploratory research on the nature of the skills the children actually have, and their relation to academic success.

Formal testing has been found to be too limited a basis for determining the language in which a child should first acquire particular skills because there are a number of factors that should be considered in making such decisions. The main concern is that the child be taught in the language in which she or he has the skills to learn, to acquire knowledge, to think creatively. Thus far it has been assumed that this should be the language in which the child is "dominant". *But a child may be dominant in one language for some topics and some social domains, but not others. Thus we see immediately that dominance is too simplistic a notion.*

From a *substantive* point of view, an ethnographic orientation entails the notion that children's school language skills should be viewed within a broader framework of culturally acquired communicative competence. While cultural differences in children's pre-school and outside of school language socialization experiences have been recognized for some ethnic minority populations in this country, notably Blacks and North American Indians, such cultural differences have been given less attention in the discussion of the educational problems of bilingual populations. For the latter group, the linguistic difference has been so salient that it has received most of the attention. In addition, there is a tendency among at least Hispanic groups to associate culture with food, dance and other very visible markers of ethnic or national identity, rather than the less displayable features of everyday culture which comprise children's socialization.

An ethnographic, and fundamentally anthropological, view of language proficiency is that the concept should embrace the child's full range of social uses of language and nonverbal signals rather than encompassing only the narrow uses associated with the transmission of the literacy skills of reading and writing. The relationship between the child's communicative skills in different domains should be examined. In this way, the knowledge of the child's communicative skills in non-academic activities might shed light on and help interpret or explain his or her patterns of language use in academic activities.

An ethnographic view of language socialization invokes "culture" and cultural differences in language socialization to explain the poor achievement scores of children from ethnic minority backgrounds. School curricula, generally, assume and build on a single model of language socialization. Sometimes there is mismatch between the school developmental model, and the child's pre-school language socialization experiences. The developmental model is based on white middle-class children's pre-school language socialization experiences, even though the ethnic minority child's language socialization is culturally different. Minority children arrive in the classroom knowing different kinds of things. When they encounter school tests, it is as if they are asked to perform "Apples" when they know "Oranges", and no one ever tests for "Oranges".

Stated quite simply, if educators are to be able to assess children's skills when they arrive at school, and if they are to be able to build on their strengths, a description of the nature of the communicative competence of children from ethnic minority backgrounds will be necessary. Educators also need to understand how cultural differences affect children's classroom behavior. In this way, when a child is having difficulties in school, educators will know if it is because the teacher and the curriculum presuppose cultural knowledge in the child that she or he doesn't have. Perhaps even the kind of knowledge that a child possesses may also be determined. In other words, an ethnographic perspective involves the advocation of the concept of culture as an explanatory tool in bilingual language proficiency assessment.

From a *methodological* point of view, an ethnographic perspective holds that experimental methodologies can never enable us to grasp the nature of children's communicative competence because such methods, by their very nature, alter that competence. Instead, observation, participant observation, and interviews are recommended as the research tools to be used in determining the nature of children's communicative competence. The place of educational testing approaches to language proficiency assessment, therefore, is within that broader perspective of communicative competence. It has also been argued that teachers can benefit from being trained to carry out ethnographic research on their students' communicative competence because it will broaden their perspective on their students' language skills, enable them to identify students' communicative strengths, and to build on those strengths and use them in academic cognitive development.

The ethnographic perspective described was used as the basis for a course on Bilingual Language Proficiency Assessment at the University of Arizona in the Spring of 1980. The course, funded by the National Institute of Education (N.I.E.) through the Assessment of Language Proficiency of Bilingual Persons (ALPBP) Project was intended as a prototype to stimulate both teaching and research on the topic of language proficiency assessment.

The objective of the course was to provide bilingual educators with information about approaches to language and language use that would be helpful in their effort to assess the "proficiency" of their students in Spanish and English. From the beginning, the course was intended to be "ethnographic" in basic orientation and emphasis, an orientation which is viewed as innovative in the area of language proficiency assessment. The course was taught from the perspective that present approaches to bilingual language proficiency assessment are inadequate and inappropriate. These inadequacies could be remedied, it was thought, in part through the joining of both theoretical/substantive and methodological aspects of ethnographic approaches to language use with the more institutionalized approaches to language proficiency assessment associated with educational psychology, and to a lesser degree, cognitive psychology.

The bilingual teachers

The course itself can be viewed as an interaction between this perspective, and my concern, as the instructor, to meet the needs of the students (teachers) in the course. Accordingly, it is appropriate to provide some information about those students and their concerns.

The students for the course were recruited through the Title VII program in the Tucson Unified School District, generally known as District One, and the Sunnyside District, also in Tucson. All but one of the students were involved in District One bilingual education programs in one way or another. Of the fifteen people who came to class the first day with an interest in enrolling in it, six were grade school classroom teachers in "full" bilingual programs. Four of these were first grade teachers, one a second grade teacher, and one a fourth grade teacher. It was to this group that the course was most directly addressed. There were also two teachers in pull-out programs for Spanish Reading who worked with Spanish dominant children in the first three grades. There was one high school teacher who worked with freshmen in a Title VII bilingual program, whose students were Mexican American, but who were learning Spanish at a beginning level. Two people in District One were in non-teaching positions associated with bilingual programs (a resource person who spent most of her time testing children and evaluating tests, and a Title VII evaluator who was also the liaison person between District One) and three administrators were from grade schools with bilingual programs. None of these last three ended up taking the course. Finally, there was one teacher who worked with learning disability students on their literacy skills in a grade school pull-out program. All but two were functionally bilingual in Spanish and English. This description well represents those who came in and out of the course, and those who finally completed the coursework.

From the first day of class, it was clear that most of the teachers were in a fairly difficult position in their roles as assessors of bilingual language proficiency. They began the school year in programs in which they had little or no "say" in determining which children were placed in bilingual programs, or which children were defined as Spanish dominant or English dominant. Most of these teachers had to administer tests designed to measure language proficiency at some point during the school year, but they usually did not receive the test scores until after the children had moved on to another grade. And most of the teachers, at some point during each year, made and acted upon decisions that could seriously affect a child's academic progress. The decisions were based on their own assessment of their students' language skills: Should a child be recommended for learning disability testing? Should he or she be transferred from the English dominant to the Spanish dominant reading group? And so on.

Generally, the teachers believed they were in a better position to assess their students' skills than others, since they were seeing them using language far more than anyone else, and, unlike many administrators, were proficient bilinguals themselves. Some of the teachers who came to this course were not only critical of the formal instruments used to measure proficiency but were skeptical about their validity. Some of the teachers showed distrust for tests used to test students for learning disabilities on the grounds that none of the formal testing instruments were in Spanish.

At the same time, none of the teachers had had any formal training in how to evaluate and interpret formal tests, so they lacked confidence in their own critical orientation. The teachers were clearly aware that their own language proficiency assessments lacked credibility with administrative personnel who made the student placement decisions with which the teachers had to live. Several teachers expressed concern over the fact that they were not consulted or that their opinions were given little attention in placement decisions that were supposed to be based on language proficiency assessments.

In general, then, the teachers came into the class with ambivalent feelings about bilingual language proficiency assessment. On the one hand, they felt their knowledge of their students' language proficiency was crucial for the child's academic development. On the other hand, they felt inadequate in their own knowledge and anxious over the decisions they *were* making.

Clearly, then, the primary practical aim of the course was to provide the teachers with information that would facilitate their language proficiency assessment activities.

The course

There were three parts to the course. Part I was an overview of approaches to bilingual language proficiency assessment, with emphasis on sociolinguistic and ethnographic approaches. Part II focused on the nature of the child's communicative competence in the classroom and the teacher's assessment of bilingual language proficiency in that context. Part III dealt with the child's communicative competence in the community and with the effects of cultural background on that competence. Each section of the course will now be considered in more detail.

Part I: Approaches to bilingual language proficiency

The primary purpose of this first five-week section was to introduce various approaches to or definitions of language proficiency that could be of use to teachers in their language proficiency assessment, and to integrate those approaches into a single coherent view. Above all, it was thought to be important to develop the notion of communicative competence as the most integrated approach to language proficiency. In addition, as the instructor I attempted to demonstrate the advantages of such a view over the more strictly linguistic notions of proficiency and the more "literacy achievement" definitions of proficiency that are most common in educational testing today.

There are three aspects of the concept of communicative competence that were highlighted in the course. First, attention was given to the point that communicative competence involves the influences of both human biological make-up and culturally acquired knowledge in the determination of the structure of language. Second, attention was given to the point that communicative competence is a combination of linguistic and social knowledge. This concept developed by Hymes (1972) refers to what a person must know to communicate in a socially appropriate fashion. The point was made that intra-linguistic diversity in dialect and style is matched by a functional differentiation in code use that could affect the nature of a child's language proficiency in two languages. The third aspect of communicative competence that was given particular emphasis in the first section of the course was the developmental process through which communicative competence was acquired. The notion of culturally specific developmental sequences was contrasted with the educational assumption implicit in curriculum materials and associated instructional booklets that there is only *one* relevant developmental sequence in terms of which children's language proficiency can be measured.

Part II: Communicative competence in the classroom

The general goal of the second part of the course was to instruct the teachers on how to carry out ethnographic observation in their classrooms, and to use that skill in increasing their awareness of the nature of their students' communicative competence in the classroom.

The means used to accomplish this goal was a research project in which the teachers were to describe their own bilingual language proficiency assessment activities, or to do an ethnographic description of their own evaluation activities and the interpretive procedures they use in assessing students' proficiency. There were no assigned readings for this section of the course, and the in-class lecture and discussion activities were organized entirely around the facilitation of this project.

In the first phase of the project, the teachers were required to provide an initial description of their language assessment procedures. Each student in the class was asked to rank a group of ten of their students in terms of their relative language proficiency in both Spanish and English. Thus, there would be two separate rankings, which could involve either the same or different children. They were asked to describe the aspects of the children's communicative competence that they attended to in making their language proficiency assessments, and the contexts within the classroom which they relied upon in making those assessments. The instructor made it clear that those in the class who were not regular classroom teachers would be able to adapt the assignment to their interests and practical circumstances.

The second phase of the project was the collection of language use data in the classroom. The teachers were asked to tape record the students they had ranked in language use activities in both Spanish and English. They were then to transcribe 10 minutes of the Spanish activity and 10 minutes of the English activity.

The third phase of the research project was the analysis of the data base in terms of the extent to which the behavioral evidence of the children's language use actually corresponded with the teacher's initial bilingual language proficiency assessment. Specifically, the teachers were to determine whether the students who had been ranked as more proficient in a given language actually displayed greater amounts in the transcripts of whatever qualities the teachers had indicated they evaluated positively. Thus, for example, if a teacher initially indicated that she used size of vocabulary of words with three or more syllables as a criterion in evaluating language proficiency, then she was to determine whether the students she had ranked as more proficient actually exhibited more than three or more syllable words in their speech more than those she viewed as less proficient.

Where the students' behavior conflicted with the teachers' initial evaluations, they were asked to indicate why they thought this had occurred. Finally, they were asked to compare their own assessments of the students' language proficiency with available scores from formal tests of language proficiency, and discuss reasons for any discrepancies between their own evaluations and those of the tests.

The primary reason for focusing on the description and evaluation of the teachers' language proficiency assessment processes was practical. The purpose of the course was to provide the teachers with knowledge and skills that would be useful to them in carrying out language proficiency assessment activities. That purpose presupposes that bilingual teachers have and should have an important role in language proficiency assessment. Yet, in practice, the teacher's role is ambiguous, as was indicated earlier. Teachers obviously have far more opportunity to assess children's language skills than other school personnel, and they continually act on those assessments in their roles as teachers. Yet many of them felt that the major academic decisions based on language proficiency assessments, such as who would be placed in what program, were out of their hands. It was clear that teachers often lacked credibility with administrators in such decisions. For example, the results of a test could be given priority over a teacher's evaluation of a child's language skills. Why they lacked credibility was not clear. This state of affairs exists in a vacuum of knowledge about what teachers actually do when they assess their students' bilingual language proficiency.

A description of the way in which teachers decide a student's proficiency in English and Spanish should be useful for a number of purposes. For the teachers, it should help them articulate to others just how they make their decisions and to substantiate these decisions in dealing with administrative personnel who doubt their abilities in this area. It should also enable teachers to more easily engage in self-evaluation of their own assessment procedures. In this way, their descriptions can be compared with those of other teachers and they can learn from one another. Such a description also enables them to compare their approaches with that offered by outside resource people, in this case, the instructor of the course.

For educational administrative personnel interested in improving bilingual language proficiency assessment procedures, such descriptive information should be useful in developing a more systematic approach to the incorporation of teacher assessment practices in the overall assessment of bilingual language proficiency. If administrative personnel agree that tests are always limited and quite specific in what they assess, and that additional sources of information should be used in making decisions that will affect students' academic experience, then the *teachers'* assessments are a natural, logical, efficient and useful source of information. Teachers' assessment procedures cannot be used systematically, however, if no one knows what they are.

For all of these reasons the teachers' research project was developed. The first paper the teachers turned in described their student rankings of Spanish and English proficiency, the *criteria* underlying those rankings, and the language use situations observed by the teacher on which those rankings were based. Then, during the week that the teachers were tape recording their classes, the instructor went over their first papers to compile a report, to be returned to the teachers, which compared their approaches so that they could learn from one another. Following is a description of the salient features identified by the teachers (most of which were reported in class):

1. Many of the criteria for language proficiency that the teachers used were very academic in orientation. Quickness of students' responses, reading comprehension, ability to grasp new concepts readily, and ability to perform tasks independently were examples of such criteria. For the teachers, then, language proficiency was merged with academic achievement to some degree. This was not surprising. In practice, probably all language proficiency assessments are situational/domain-specific. Since a teacher's main professional function is the evaluation of academic progress, it is appropriate that those aspects of language use which reflect academic achievement should be salient in their conscious discriminations.

2. Most of the teachers identified features of linguistic structure among the dimensions of language use relied on in making language proficiency assessments. Syntax and vocabulary were most often mentioned as aspects attended to. Examples were too infrequent for it to be clear how these features were measured, but assessment included the notions that the larger the vocabulary, the greater the use of synonyms, and the less recourse to the other language, the more proficiency. Proper word order, particularly having the adjective before the noun in English and after the noun in Spanish, was one syntactic criterion teachers mentioned in class. Correct use of verb tenses and syntactic complexity were also mentioned. No teacher mentioned pronunciation as a factor in these papers. Greater fluency was also taken as evidence of greater proficiency in both Spanish and English.

3. There were several often-mentioned aspects of language use that were specific to the assessment of *bilingual* as opposed to monolingual language proficiency. Code-switching or mixing of language was mentioned repeatedly as evidence of *less* language proficiency. While the teachers recognized the social genesis of code-switching and did not view it as stigmatized, all of them were committed to programs in which Spanish and English were kept separate, so that for any given lesson, or participant structure, their intent was to use only one language for the entire activity. Thus,

while their students entered their bilingual programs with much mixing of languages, the teachers made it clear that the students were to try to stay in the one language in which the teacher initiated the learning activity. Given this approach, switches into the "other" language were interpreted by the teacher as evidence of lesser control of the language of the lesson.

The teachers also repeatedly mentioned "the language of the home" as a dimension of their assessment process. In other words, if the teacher knew that Spanish was spoken in the student's home, she was likely to attribute more proficiency in Spanish to him or her. This aspect of language use was set aside until Part III of the course.

4. Most of the teachers indicated that they relied almost exclusively on organized lesson activities in which they controlled the interaction as the contextual basis for their language proficiency assessments. All of the grade school teachers relied particularly heavily on *reading group activity*. Only two teachers gave systematic attention to contextual variation in children's language proficiency. In their discussions, however, and more informally in other reports, there was discussion of contextual variation in amount of student talk, presaging the emergence of "amount of talk" as an important variable in bilingual language proficiency assessment. Two patterns of assessment were evident in this realm. First, some teachers indicated that they were uncertain about the proficiency of their lowest ranked students because the children spoke so little that it was difficult to evaluate them. Second, some teachers indicated that they had students who spoke very little when the whole class met with the teacher as a group where participation was voluntary, but were proficiently responsive in small groups where everyone was expected to take a turn. Because of this second pattern, the teachers were unwilling to associate lack of talk with lack of proficiency and felt this second group may get unrepresentative scores on oral language proficiency tests.

5. On the basis of the teachers' descriptions and the instructor's observations in six of the teachers' bilingual classrooms, it became evident that *there is rarely if ever complete functional equivalence between Spanish and English in such classrooms*. The two languages are always to some degree used for different purposes.

The most common pattern in the early grades was this: The school day began with the whole class meeting with the teacher, and the activities of this time (Pledge of Allegiance, calendar review, roll call, announcements) were alternately in Spanish and English, with alternate days or weeks for each. The reading groups were either always in Spanish or always in English, with brief stilted forays into the other language through ESL (English as a Second Language) or SSL (Spanish as a Second Language) that most of the teachers viewed as ineffective. This should cause the educator to question whether the transfer of reading skills from Spanish to English can be matched by a transfer of the *verbal* language use skills associated with reading groups. Mathematics was the academic activity most likely to involve preview /review alternation in both languages, but here, too, some teachers reported staying in one language. All the teachers seemed to have a better sense of the students' competence in *one* language, usually Spanish, than in the other, and they made this clear in their descriptions.

It was apparent that the teachers taking the course were overwhelmed with the research project as a whole. The two main concerns were that they were being asked to perform tasks in areas that they felt lacking in the skill and knowledge, and that the project required too much time and energy. It was felt to be too much work. Thus I developed a final format for the analysis of the taped transcripts that was more structured and limited in form than had been originally intended: Rather than requiring the teachers to operationalize their own criteria (e.g. decide what constituted evidence in the transcript of good oral reading or verbal fluency or complex syntax), the instructor selected and operationalized most of the criteria to be examined. The components of the project as it was executed were the following.

First, the teachers were asked to look at two features in both English and Spanish from the *Bilingual Syntax Measure (BSM)* (Burt, Dulay, & Hernández-Chávez, 1975). For each language, one feature that was thought to be acquired relatively early was used (presence of articles, e.g. la, el; the, a) along with one feature acquired relatively late (direct and indirect object pronouns in Spanish, and the past Irregular tense for verbs in English). These particular features were also chosen because it was expected that they would occur relatively frequently. The teachers were asked to give the number of "correct" uses of these features in relation to the number of instances where they should have occurred.

There were several general reasons for drawing features from the *BSM:*

— the test is based on syntactic features, and a number of the teachers had said they attend to syntax in making language proficiency assessments;
— it seemed that use of the test features would facilitate comparison of test features with teacher-identified features. Use of such features would also facilitate discussion of their occurrence in a test situation compared with their occurrence in ordinary classroom interaction.

Because the teachers had expressed so much uncertainty over the assignment and viewed it as too difficult, it seemed important to give them some features that would be easy to identify and easy to count in their transcriptions. Thus a second component of the assignment was that they examine the frequency of their students' code-switching in both Spanish and English. This feature of students' language use was identified by the teachers as one they rely on in language proficiency assessments, and because this aspect of language use is distinctive to bilingual language proficiency assessment, it seemed an appropriate variable to examine for this course.

Third, the class as a group was given a choice from among four possible features that they had identified as relevant in their first papers, and that the instructor had judged to be readily defineable. From among these, the class members identified *fluency* of speech as the feature they felt was most promising. As a group, they agreed to focus on "false starts" as the aspect of fluency to be examined in their transcripts, and as a group they developed a more precise definition of false starts.

Finally, the teachers were to select one linguistic feature they had identified that they felt was particularly promising and that could be defined in such a way that others could recognize it and count it.

There were several reasons for the emphasis on operationalization of features of students' language use and quantification of behavioral differences among the students. First, as noted earlier, one purpose of the second part of the course was to compare teacher language proficiency assessment with the assessment format of tests. If quantified, the teacher's foci of evaluation and relative ranking of students could be more directly compared with those of the tests. Second, it seemed important to determine whether the teachers could explain to others what they do in a way that would enable others to look at the same aspects of language use that the teachers look at, and thus evaluate and systematically incorporate teacher assessment procedures into routine language assessment in the schools.

During the third part of the course, I provided the teachers with a summary of their Part II final analyses.

Most of the teachers, who recorded their students, taped and transcribed them in reading groups, usually in Spanish. The heavy use of reading groups was partly motivated by the fact that this is probably the main situation in which oral language use is assessed by teachers. The second reason for use of reading groups is that it can be taped and the tape transcribed more readily than many other classroom activities. Also, the teachers had been urged to consider such factors in selecting activities to tape.

In the first part of the final analyses, the teachers were asked to compare the results of their analyses of their students' language use with the achievement scores found in the students' records. The teachers found the records to be poor and incomplete. Some could find no such information for their first grade level students. The scores available to the different teachers were from different tests, making it clear that there was no standardization in testing in the school district. None of the teachers found an absolute correlation between their own initial rankings of their students and the results of language proficiency tests, although there was a general correlation. Conflicting rankings were usually in the top half of the groups of students in questions and most commonly involved one child who talked a lot. This child was often evaluated more highly by the teacher than by the test.

None of the teachers attempted to explain discrepancies between the tests and their own rankings.

Those who completed their assignments rejected the features from the *Bilingual Syntax Measure* (Burt *et al.*, 1975) as useless for their purposes, just as they had been very critical of the test when it was discussed earlier in class. Generally they said the features in both Spanish and English were completely or almost completely controlled by all of their students, including all of the students at the first grade level. Interestingly enough, they all also found that direct and indirect pronouns occurred too infrequently in their material to be effectively evaluated, suggesting that whatever utterance types normally display pronouns in Spanish are not being generated by reading group discussions. The suggestion of one teacher that English verb tenses in general rather than the Past Irregular be considered as a useful indicator of linguistic control was supported by the others in the class in class discussion.

The discussions of the variable of *code-switching* as an indicator of lesser proficiency were among the most interesting in the teachers' final analyses. None of them concluded that this dimension of language functioned as they had initially expected it to. Some members of the class arrived at the opinion that there was *more* code-switching among the students they had ranked as most proficient in a given language rather than less. Class discussion of this finding indicated that students with good code-switching skills are generally perceived by the teachers as particularly competent or naturally gifted in language skills.

I informed the teachers that comparison of the different papers and transcripts indicated that there was more code-switching from Spanish into English than from English into Spanish. Transcripts and observations from five different first grade classes indicated that in both languages the amount of code-switching done by the students was roughly proportional to the amount of code-switching done by the teacher. In other words, in classes where the students switched a lot, so did the teacher. In classes where the students switched not at all, neither did the teacher. It is not clear who was conditioning whom in such activity.

The teachers also rejected fluency as an indicator of greater control of the language in question. The two first grade teachers who finished their analyses independently concluded that disfluencies in the form of false starts were associated with longer turns at talk and more complex utterances, which in turn were produced by the students the teachers had judged to be the most proficient. This finding led the members of the class to agree that *turn length* and *utterance complexity* might be good features of language to examine in future work of this kind.

In general, the teachers were more enthusiastic about the utility of the features of language use that they had chosen on their own than those I suggested or those selected by the group. These features included errors in oral reading, number of student responses acknowledged and evaluated positively by the teacher, amount of talk (by number of turns, number of words, and number of syllables), correctness of all verb forms, and number of words with three or more syllables. The teachers who measured performance according to *reading* skills and *positive teacher evaluations* found the strongest correlations with their own rankings, providing further evidence of the extent to which language proficiency and academic achievement are merged in the teachers' language proficiency assessments.

Those who looked at amount of talk did not find it to correlate with their rankings, primarily because there was usually one exception to the correlation. But my perusal of reports and transcripts taken as a body suggest that, in fact, there is a very strong general correlation between amount of talk and positive or high language proficiency assessment of a student.

Concluding remarks

The teachers seemed to feel that their awareness of the ways students use language had been heightened by the project activities and that their own intuitions about their students' use of language were only born out some of the time when their students' language use was examined more closely. The experience did not cause them to question their own rankings. Instead, where students' performance in terms of the teachers' own criteria was not what the teachers expected, they tended to criticize the use of those criteria and the methodology of the research project. They believed they were working with too little data to be able to confirm or eliminate the features examined. I also shared this view but to a lesser degree since I had access to all the papers and the data. It was also clear that the features examined interact with other features not examined in complex and subtle ways.

This experience suggests that it is generally quite difficult to operationalize the teacher assessment processes. If teacher judgements are more systematically used in making student program decisions in the future, it will probably be necessary to accept the *qualitative* nature of their judgements.

It is also clear that the teachers' basis for making language proficiency assessments is, in fact, almost always limited to the academic activities which the teacher alone controls. The expansion of that base to other sources of information was the focus of the third part of the course.

Part III: Communicative competence in the community

The general purpose of this third part of the course was to facilitate the teachers' exploration of sources of information on their students' communicative competence that they do not normally use as a basis for making bilingual language proficiency assessments. As in the second part of the course, the teachers were given an empirical research project to carry out involving gathering of additional information on the same students they had ranked in the first project. Once again, the inclass activities were designed to acquaint the teachers with approaches that would help them in their projects. This time, however, the project was less structured, allowing the teachers to decide how much time to devote to it, and readings were assigned to accompany the inclass lectures and discussion.

Basically, the teachers were asked to consider whether access to a broadened view of their students' communicative competence would give them insight into the students' inclass language use and/or alter the nature of the teachers' rankings of their students' bilingual language proficiency.

The third part of the course was designed to broaden their view of their students' communicative competence in two ways:

— They were to consider the nature of contextual variation in children's communicative competence, considering how the children communicated in school contexts which the teachers did not normally observe, and in community contexts. In general, then, they were to relate the children's performance in academic activities to a larger pattern of communicative skills.
— The second way in which the third section of the course was to broaden the teachers' views of their children's communicative competence was through consideration of the relationship between the students' social backgrounds and their language proficiency as it had been assessed by the teacher on the basis of academic activities.

While the Part III assignment encouraged the teachers to consider a number of sources of information, problems with the Anthropology Department Human Subjects Committee made it necessary to ask them not to make visits to students' homes to gather information or gather information from their school files. Thus, in their assessment, they were limited to observation and tape recording of activities taking place on the school grounds, and to information that they had acquired about the children during their normal teaching activities. Those who had already gathered additional background information from other sources before this restriction was made were allowed to go ahead and use that information in their final papers.

Of the five people taking the course who reported on the Part III assignment, three concentrated on observation of their students in contexts where they did not normally see them and two concentrated on the relationship between features of the students' social backgrounds and their language proficiency in Spanish and English. Their general evaluation of this project was that it was very useful to carry out such activities, and that one gained insight into the nature of the children's communicative skills that could not be gained through regular classroom activities.

Two of the teachers who observed the students in activities on the school grounds found a general correlation between the students' amount of talk in these situations and in the classroom. More particularly, they found that the students they had ranked as least proficient in at least one language were loners outside the classroom, and weren't talking because they weren't with anyone. One person taking the course found a child who used Spanish little in the classroom, even when addressed in Spanish, but relied on it heavily in interaction with peers in the cafeteria, making plausible the notion that some students see the classroom as a place for English, no matter what kind of program they are in.

The teachers agreed that observation of students in activities not controlled by the teacher should be a regular part of bilingual language proficiency assessment. However, they felt that in order for it to be practical, it would be best to recommend that teachers observe students in unsupervised activity in the classroom. They found the cafeteria to be an excellent situation for observation, but felt some teachers would find it a burden to be required to observe there. They found the playground a very poor place to observe, because of the level of activity of the children.

The teachers who looked at the correlation between language proficiency and social background were surprised by several of their findings. One teacher who taught Spanish as a second language to Mexican-American students at the high school level found that there was a strong correlation between the students' identification of Spanish as their first language, and her positive assessments of their present Spanish proficiency. In other words, her "good" students were those who had been exposed to Spanish early, and/or had had it and lost it. Another teacher, who taught at the first grade level found that there was a strong correlation between high proficiency in Spanish, and birth in Mexico, and between high proficiency in English, and birth in the United States. While this correlation might seem obvious, it has apparently been disputed among those working in Tucson in bilingual education. This same teacher found a strong correlation between students' birth order position and proficiency in a language. Those who were first-born in their family tended to be ranked as more proficient in both languages by this teacher. The other teachers strongly agreed that this factor is a very promising one for explaining differences in language proficiency. However, although the teachers found social background information helped them explain patterns in their students' communicative competence, they did not feel that teachers should regularly have access to such information, or be encouraged to use it in making placement decisions. They felt that such information might tend to bias the assessment of a child's abilities, so that e.g. a child who was from Mexico and fourth-born would be assumed to have little English proficiency.

On the last day of class, the teachers were given copies of transcripts of tape recordings from a bilingual second grade class whose teacher was not taking the course. Two transcripts in English involved students ranked as fifth (E-5) and tenth (E-10) in a group of ten in English skills by their teacher. In one situation that was recorded, the students read aloud in a reading group. In the other the students were at a learning center developing menus of food, unsupervised by a teacher. The teachers were impressed by the variety of forms of speech that appeared in the two transcripts, and felt that the great range of language skills exposed by the situational contrast argued strongly for regular observation of students in diverse activities, as a regular part of bilingual language proficiency assessment procedures.

Another group of teachers who examined the same pair of transcripts showed a high level of agreement in choosing which speaker showed the greater proficiency (E10). The teachers' assessments were consistent with the child's teacher's ranking but varied in the criteria they used to arrive at their decision.

The main sources of evidence of language skills in the reading lesson are the child's reading aloud and his or her answers to the teacher's questions about the material read. In that transcript, some teachers considered frequency and type of reading error as a basis for comparing E5 and E10, and found them to differ in both aspects. Speed and frequency of response to questions, as well as richness of vocabulary in the responses were also considered. In many teachers' judgments E10's language skills in reading and responses to questions were clearly superior.

The difference emerges more clearly when the two children were recorded at the learning center. There the teacher does not control turns at talk, and E10 talks a great deal more than E5. E10 controls the interaction and also engages in some verbal play toward the end of the transcript. Here, too, the teachers judged E10 as demonstrating greater English language proficiency.

Recommendations for teacher training

Teachers in all classrooms are continually making assessments of their students' language proficiencies, and incorporating those assessments into decisions about the kinds of learning activities the students will be involved in. Until recently, the principal form of training that teachers have been given in language awareness was derived from the traditional prescriptive grammatical approach that preceded the treatment of language by modern linguists.

There are several areas of knowledge about language from which all teachers could benefit in their language proficiency assessment activities. Teachers' language arts activities would be strengthened by a general background on the structure of language, and on its inherent rule-governed variability. Such a background would give them the tools to describe and analyze the forms of speech of their students, for their own benefit and that of other school personnel involved in placement decisions. It would also give them the analytical tools to take a less evaluative attitude toward particular varieties of language that reflect patterned variation, but tend to be stigmatized in evaluations of language. A general introduction to sociolinguistic characterizations of the relation between the social life of the child and his or her way of speaking would also sensitize teachers to the cultural foundations upon which they can build in developing their students' language skills.

For those who teach in bilingual programs, there is also a need for in-depth familiarization with standard texts used in assessing bilingual language proficiency, and with their strengths and weaknesses. And as long as these tests continue to be limited in what they can tell us about the skills of bilingual children, there will also be a need for teachers to receive further training that will allow them to systematically supplement test knowledge with direct observation of their students' language use. This training could, in turn, be related to knowledge of the ways in which bilingual children use language in community environments. A course such as the one described here can be very useful in meeting this final need.

References

Bilingual Education Act of 1968: Title VII ESEA. In S. Schneider, *Revolution, reaction, or reform: The 1974 Bilingual Education Act.* New York: L.A. Publishing Co. Inc. 1976.

Burt, M. K., Dulay, H. C. & Hernández-Chávez, E. 1975, *Bilingual syntax measure: Manual.* New York: Harcourt-Brace-Jovanovich Inc.

Civil Rights Act of 1964 42 U.S.C. 2000d.

Hymes, D. 1972, On communicative competence. In J.B. Pride & J. Holmes (eds), *Sociolinguistics.* Harmondsworth, Middlesex: Penguin.

Teacher training and ethnographic/sociolinguistic issues in the assessment of bilingual students' language proficiency[1]

Carmen Simich-Dudgeon
Georgetown University
Washington, D.C.

Charlene Rivera[2]
Information Systems Consultants Inc.
Bethesda, MD

Traditionally, schools have used a developmental model of acquisition of communicative skills based on white middle-class children's socialization experiences. This model assumes all children come to school having the same basic experiences at home and in the community. It also assumes that cognitive and linguistic skill development follows a rather fixed growth curve which takes as the norm white middle-class children's developmental characteristics. These assumptions are reflected in standard monolingual curriculum objectives as well as in the segmentation of knowledge by grade level. The model fails to recognize culturally different language socialization experiences. This model assumes all children come to school having the same lacks the necessary flexibility to build upon variability in the acquisition of communicative skills by children of different cultural backgrounds, and to relate these skills to the learning of new concepts at school. This lack of understanding and acceptance of culturally different language socialization patterns of communication may be a major factor contributing to the poor performance in school by language minority students (see Philips article, this volume).

In view of the inadequacies of this model and in an effort to explore alternative methods for assessing language proficiency, a two year teacher training program was implemented through the Assessment of Language Proficiency of Bilingual Persons (ALPBP) project. The training consisted in the instruction of target teachers in ethnographic/sociolinguistic approaches to communicative proficiency and its assessment.

The approach entails both theoretical and methodological considerations about the nature of children's language acquisition, language use and its measurement.

Theoretical and methodological approach

From a theoretical perspective, the concept of language proficiency is seen as embracing "the child's full range of social uses of language and non-verbal signals rather than encompassing only the narrow uses associated with the transmission of literacy skills of reading and writing" (see Philips, this volume p. 89).

In order to operationalize this interpretation of the language construct, Briere's (1979) integrative model of communicative proficiency was modified for use in the training process to include those developmental factors which influence children's language development and language use. The model, illustrated in Figure 1, consists of four basic components: linguistic competence and linguistic performance — based on Chomsky's (1965) understanding of language — and sociolinguistic competence and sociolinguistic performance — based on Hymes (1972) interpretation of communicative competence.

Linguistic competence refers to the intuitive knowledge a native speaker has about the rules of the grammar of his/her language(s) (i.e. phonology, syntax, and the lexicon). This refers, for example, to the tacit knowledge a native English-speaking student has about when and how to use both regular and irregular plurals, to make verb and noun agreements, or to understand the sounds of the dialectal variations spoken in various communities.

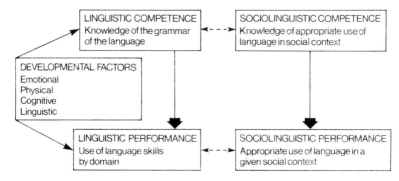

FIGURE 1. *A sociolinguistic/linguistic model of communicative proficiency (Adapted from Briere, 1979)*

Linguistic performance refers to the actual use the speaker makes of his/her linguistic competence using the "proper" grammar and vocabulary. These skills are evidenced in the ability to comprehend and speak as well as to read and write if literacy skills have been introduced.

Sociolinguistic competence refers to the knowledge a native speaker has about the appropriate use of his/her language within different social environments, i.e. the tacit knowledge of what to say to whom, for what reason(s) and under what circumstance(s). In the school setting, it refers to the knowledge a student has of the appropriate rules of interaction and interpretation when interacting with teachers, peers and other participants.

Sociolinguistic performance refers to the actual communicative behaviors of a speaker which lead other members of a speech community to believe that he/she is communicating appropriately. For example, in U.S. schools teachers often expect students to look them in the eye while being reprimanded or when responding. In some cultures this is considered inappropriate; thus, if a student does not provide a response appropriate to the culture, a teacher unfamiliar with the child's cultural background might conclude that the student is disrespectful or uncooperative.

The ethnographic perspective requires the application of methodologies which support observation of naturally occurring interactions, participant observations and interviews as research tools for determining the nature of children's communicative proficiency. This is in contrast to experimental methodologies which focus on language interactions in contrived rather than natural settings. By their very nature, experimental methodologies disregard children's natural language abilities because they focus on knowledge of language skills which may lie outside their socialization experiences.

In an effort to develop observational criteria to be used in analyzing observations of children's naturally occurring communicative interactions and relate these to communicative proficiency, ALPBP project staff reviewed current theoretical and applied research on the nature of language and its functional uses. Following is a brief summary from that review.

Hymes (1964) argues that knowledge of a language implies more than an innate and subconscious knowledge of the rules of the language (Chomsky, 1965). He suggests that language use within a speech community consists of culturally influenced communication modes, which include systematic patterning of speech governed by social rules. He proposes that an ethnography of speaking is required to describe the patterns of language use in terms of their distribution and *function*. He categorizes language in terms of basic functions: expressive, directive and referential.

Halliday (1973) categorizes language functions as instrumental, regulatory, interactional, heuristic, personal, imaginative and representational. The instrumental function, according to Halliday, serves to manipulate the environment, to cause certain events to happen, such as "don't touch the stove!" etc. The regulatory function serves in controlling events through the use of approval, disapproval, etc. The representational function refers to the use of language to make statements, convey facts and knowledge, such as to explain, or to report, etc. The interactional function serves to ensure social maintenance. This is exhibited in knowledge of slang, jargon, jokes, politeness and formality expectations. The personal function allows a speaker to express feelings and emotions. The heuristic function involves language used to acquire knowledge and to learn about the environment. Heuristic functions are often conveyed in the form of questions that will lead to answers. Children make good use of the heuristic functions in their use of *why* questions. The imaginative functions serve to create imaginary systems of ideas, such as telling fairy tales, writing novels, creating poetry, etc.

Tough (1974) considers two basic functions of language: relational and ideational. The first one is used to "maintain the self" and the second is used to direct one's self to others' actions.

Wilkinson (1975) developed a list of language functions as a result of ethnographic/sociolinguistic observations of young children's communicative interactions. Because of their importance in understanding the language use by school children, the functions are listed below.

Functions of language

Who am I?	1	Establishing and maintaining self
	2	Language for analyzing self
	3	Language for expressing self
		(for celebrating or despairing, etc.)
Who are you?	4	Establishing and maintaining relations
	5	Co-operating
	6	Empathizing, understanding the other
	7	Role playing, mimicry
	8	Guiding, directing the other
Who/What is	9	Giving information
he/she/it?	10	Recalling events (past)
	11	Describing present events
	12	Predicting future events —
		statements of intention
		statements of hypothesis
		what might happen

13 Analyzing, classifying
14 Explaining, giving reason for
15 Exploring, asking questions, but in other ways also, by "sounding out" people
16 Reflecting on own/others' thoughts and feelings
(Wilkinson, 1975, pp. 56–7)

In her study of teacher/children's language interactions, Fillmore (1979) suggests several functions of language related to children's production and comprehension. Samples of functions which she recognizes as important during classroom interactions are: to provide and elicit information, to explain, to describe, to clarify, etc.

In addition to research on language functions, psycholinguistic research by Cummins was felt to be important to the study of children's language use in school. Cummins (1980) suggests that there are two independent dimensions of language proficiency: cognitive-academic language skills, which are related to literacy skills, and sociolinguistic language skills, which are related to interpersonal communication skills.

Fillmore's (1976) research on the acquisition of English skills of five early elementary school children indicates that both aspects of language proficiency suggested by Cummins have unique but inter-related characteristics. Both are essential for successful achievement and social interaction in the classroom. Fillmore notes that sociolinguistic aspects of language are crucial to the acquisition and development of a second language in early elementary school children while cognitive-related functions often become more critical for older second-language learners because of the emphasis on academic performance at higher grade levels. The implication of Fillmore's work is that both sociolinguistic and cognitive-academic language aspects are important to meaningful and appropriate communication of second language learners.

More recent research on language use in the classroom suggests that there are two dichotomous language dimensions. One is more related to the service of cognition — academic-related language functions — and the other is related to the service of interpersonal social interactions — socio-affective related language functions (Genesee, 1983). Successful communication with other participants seems to be correlated to the degree to which the individual has mastered both dimensions of language use.

Implementation of the ALPBP teacher training program: processes and outcomes

The insights gained from the literature together with our experience as educators of language minority students provided the basis for developing a framework for training teachers in the Tucson Unified School District (TUSD) in language proficiency assessment issues utilizing ethnographic/sociolinguistic methodologies. Because of the district's interest in the development of innovative approaches to the education of language minority students TUSD was selected as the training site.

TUSD serves a community in excess of 500,000. Approximately 57,000 students are enrolled in TUSD schools. Approximately 16,000, or 28.4 percent, are Hispanic, of which approximately 11,000 have been identified as having a primary language other than English. In addition, the school district also services about 1,000 students from 79 various language backgrounds.

TUSD administrators felt that the ALPBP teacher training program in ethnographic/sociolinguistic methodologies would complement their efforts in developing a non-traditional language proficiency assessment instrument, the *Language Proficiency Measure (LPM)* (TUSD, 1981). The educators who became involved in the training program were teachers and administrators from the school district. The process of establishing a relationship with TUSD administrators and teachers took place over approximately a six month period in the fall and winter of 1979. District administrators provided input into the content of the program during the planning stage through a variety of phone conversations and on-site meetings. Teachers had an opportunity to contribute to the training plan through a needs assessment survey and formal and informal meetings.

The general goal of the training component of the ALPBP project was to provide a forum wherein teachers and administrators would explore the application of ethnographic/sociolinguistic theories and methodologies applied to language proficiency assessment practices. The expected outcome of the training was that it would enable Tucson educators to develop more effective language proficiency assessment strategies applicable to their particular student population. The actual training which was implemented in three phases is described below.

Phase I: Bilingual language proficiency assessment: an ethnographic approach

Phase I of the ALPBP teacher training program was implemented in the spring of 1980 by Dr. Susan Philips through an agreement with the University of Arizona School of Education Bilingual Program and the College of Liberal Arts Anthropology Department to co-sponsor a three credit (45 hr.) graduate course. The course, "An Ethnographic Approach to

Bilingual Language Proficiency Assessment," was developed to meet the needs of participating teachers. It focused on three aspects of language proficiency as they relate to language minority students:

— Models of Language Proficiency;
— Language Proficiency in the Bilingual Classroom; and
— Language Proficiency in the Bilingual Community.

Through the course teachers were provided with background in approaches to the assessment of language proficiency of language minority students. They were introduced to basic sociolinguistic and ethnographic concepts related to language assessment, and were guided in the exploration of the nature of children's language proficiency in both classroom and community contexts. Sources of information included lectures, readings and discussions and student projects. A more detailed description of this aspect of the training component is found in Philips' chapter in this book, "An Ethnographic Approach to Language Proficiency Assessment".

Phase II: Development of a student observation instrument to determine the communicative proficiency of language minority students
The theoretical and methodological issues introduced by Philips formed the basis for development of Phase II, which took the form of a three-week intensive workshop. The goal of the workshop was to provide the participants with practical ethnographic/sociolinguistic field techniques which would enable them to participate in the development of a student observation instrument. With the instructors' guidance — Carmen Simich, a sociolinguist, and Robert Carrasco, an ethnographer — participants developed the *Teacher Observation System TOS.*
The workshop included a review of the basic concepts of ethnographic monitoring in classroom settings. Videotapes of interactions between teacher/student(s) and student(s)/student(s) in elementary bilingual classrooms were used to aid the development of teachers' observation skills. The process was one of guided discovery where, through discussion and brainstorming, teachers were made aware of the wide range of communicative skills students use with different participants in various classroom situations. The videotapes provided a means for detailed discussion of teacher/student(s) interactions vs. student(s)/student(s) interactions which focused on:

— language use, language choice, code-switching and their relationship to communicative proficiency;

— students' linguistic repertoires; and
— sociolinguistic rules of interaction in the classroom.

The discussions resulting from viewing the videotapes were related to the teachers' practical experience as ethnographers and participant observers. After viewing the tapes, the participants and workshop leaders agreed that teachers were the most qualified to make valid emic predictions about their own students' communicative abilities. Outside observers, it was concurred, would not generally be aware of the specific rules of interaction implicitly or explicitly agreed upon by participants in classroom settings.

Early in the workshop, teachers were asked to list students' behaviors that, in their opinion, correlated with English proficiency. The purpose of the activity was to identify participants' understanding of communicative proficiency. Responses from this informal survey, summarized in Table 1, were analyzed, and grouped into four categories of behaviors. These are:

— linguistic behaviors related to grammatical, morphological and syntactic skills in oral speech, as well as literacy skills;
— ethnographic/sociolinguistic behaviors related to language use considering setting, participants, nonverbal behaviors, goals of interaction, language(s) used by students;
— student background factors related to language of the home, language(s) exposure, years of schooling, etc.; and
— psychological factors related to self-concept and language(s) used in emotional interactions.

TABLE 1 *Teacher selected factors used to evaluate students' communicative proficiency*

Linguistic behaviors	Number of times selected	Percentage
Speaking		
Code-switching (using two languages during discourse)	5	
Use of dialect(s)	1	
"Good" pronunciation	1	
Responding "well" to directions, questions, etc.	1	
Initiating conversation	2	
Contributing to discussion	4	
Ability to explain in a group situation (e.g. "good" productive ability, amount of talk, ability to negotiate)	15	

Writing
Word order, noun and verb agreement, placement of
   adjective before noun   5
"Satisfactorily" completing writing assignments in
   English   2
Completing tasks independently and accurately,
   "with 'good' control of syntax and vocabulary"   4
Building on sentences   2

Listening
"Good" receptive ability   5
Understanding verbal cues   2

Reading
Reading on grade level   1
   Total number of times selected   50   65

Ethnographic/Sociolinguistic Behaviors

Language(s) used with peers during unsupervised
   play situations   4
Language(s) used with peers and teacher during supervised
   situations   1
Ability to initiate conversation with teacher and peers
   in classroom in both small and large instructional
   groups   2
Use of jingles during unsupervised activities in the
   playground   1
Language fluency   2
Nonverbal behaviors (e.g. "responds by nodding,
   blank look, head down")   3
   Total number of times selected   13   17

Students' background factors

Language(s) spoken at home   5
Language used most frequently by student at home   1
Information in students' cummulative file   1
Number of years of schooling   1
Ethnic background   1
   Total number of times selected   9   12

Psychological factors

Student is "shy or self conscious"   4
Language(s) used in emotional interactions   1
   Total number of times selected   5   6

Total number of factors   77

Sixty-five per cent of the total number of behaviors identified were linguistic, 17 per cent fell within the ethnographic/sociolinguistic category, 12 per cent were student background factors and 6 per cent were psychological factors. The most frequently cited linguistic behaviors focused on ability to explain, amount of code-switching during discourse, contribution to discussion and initiating conversation. Word order, command of syntax, and vocabulary as well as the ability to complete writing assignments were cited as major indicators of "good" writing ability. Listening factors selected were "good" receptive ability and understanding verbal cues. Only one reading skill, the ability to read at grade level, was named.

   Among the most often listed ethnographic/sociolinguistic behaviors were: the language(s) students use during play situations, the use of nonverbal behaviors, "language fluency," and ability to initiate conversation with different participants in distinct contextual settings. Background information factors cited were: language of the home, number of years of schooling, information in students' cumulative files, and ethnic background. Language use in the home was the one most often mentioned. The psychological factors designated were: students' shyness or self-consciousness, and language(s) used during emotional interactions. In short, results from the survey indicated that:

— teachers' criteria for judging language proficiency is generally based on a consideration of linguistic factors with a particular emphasis on oral language skills;
— few teachers include nonverbal language in their criteria of communicative performance; and
— few teachers consider, in their criteria, students' appropriate use of language in terms of contextual and psychological factors affecting communication.

   The communicative proficiency model adapted from Briere (1979, see Figure 1) was discussed with teachers, and related to results from the teacher survey. The purpose in utilizing this model was to make participants aware that language use requires speakers/listeners to possess more than the knowledge of the grammar of a language and that sociolinguistic aspects of language should be taken into account when assessing communicative proficiency. After relating the model to the results of the survey, participants arrived at the conclusion that there was a need to consider the communicative proficiency of their students in terms of both linguistic *and* sociolinguistic skills.

The review of basic ethnographic concepts, discussion of the results from the teachers' survey of communicative proficiency factors, and a modified sociolinguistic model of communicative proficiency (Briere, 1979) provided the foundation for the inductive process used to develop the *TOS*.

The major questions raised during its conceptualization and development were:

— What kinds of functional language skills does the language minority student bring to school?
— In which language(s), social contexts, and for what purposes does the student communicate best?
— In which language(s) does the student have the widest contextual range of communicative abilities?
— What kinds of communicative skills does the student need to master in order to participate appropriately as a member of the school speech community?

Important in the process of developing the *TOS* was the selection of contextual settings in which to observe students' communicative interactions, the language(s) of instruction, directness or indirectness of "teacher talk", and classroom organization (teacher-centered vs. student-centered). The language characteristics and linguistic background of the student were also considered consequential for planning of the *TOS*. Ethnographic, sociolinguistic and educational variables considered significant were: background of parents, number of siblings at home, age, language use at home and in the community, ethnohistorical and ethnolinguistic information.

The recognition that students have varied repertoires of functional language use in different situations and with different participants, motivated the selection of some components of speech events suggested by Hymes (1972) as the basis for developing the *TOS*. Table 2 describes those components used during the initial stage of development. They were: setting, participants, channel of communication, languages used and discourse characteristics.

Ideally, an ethnographic approach to language proficiency assessment consists of observing a student in the community, home and school contexts. However, because of the impracticability of doing so in all three concepts, it was decided to obtain community and home information through student interviews and other available school records, and to observe students only in the school setting.

TABLE 2 *Components of instructional events to be considered in the development of the Teacher Observation System*

Setting	Participants	Channels of communication	Language(s) used	Discourse characteristics
Instructional (formal) vs. Non-instructional (Informal) events	Teacher/Student(s) Student/Student(s)	speaking listening reading writing	English Spanish	coherence complexity adequacy of vocabulary code-switching

The advantages and disadvantages of using the categories of setting, participant(s), sociolinguistic behaviors, etc., was a critical issue of discussion in the development of the *TOS*. After considering the range of speech events that usually occur in a school day, three representative situations and social contexts were chosen. In order to assist observers in the description of students' communicative behavior in the different interactional contexts, basic questions were developed. The questions provide a guide to the observer in describing a student's range of communicative skills. The questions and interactions are described in Table 3.

TABLE 3 *Observation questions in social contexts*

Social contexts:	Adult directed instructional	Peer group instructional	Non-instructional	Other
Questions to be answered during observations	1. What language(s) and/or nonverbal behavior are used by the student to communicate? When the child does not communicate verbally, what evidence do you see that indicates understanding? Describe the behavior observed. 2. When the student does not seem to understand, what does she/he do to clarify the situation? Describe the communicative behavior observed. 3. Does the student follow the implicit and explicit rules of communication of the social context you are observing?			

The field test version of the *TOS* (Appendix A) has three components:

Section I: Background Information
Section II: Teacher Observation Data Sheet
Section III: Description of Observation Data

Section I consists of a three part questionnaire: student information, optimal student information, and teacher information. The first part includes questions regarding basic information about a student's name, age, sex, birthdate and language usage. The second part contains questions about previous schooling experiences and language(s) used in the home. The third part includes questions about the teacher's language background. Section II includes four social contexts used to describe students' communicative behavior. Three basic questions guide the observer to focus on specific communicative behavior. Section III consists of two parts. In part one, the teacher summarizes the observed student's communicative behavior. In part two, extralinguistic factors that may affect students' communicative ability (e.g. physical, emotional, and/or social) are described.

A Manual for use with the *TOS* was also developed. It consists of four sections:

— Introduction
— Rationale: description of the ethnographic/sociolinguistic theories and methodologies underlying the development of the *TOS*
— How to use the *TOS*
— Glossary of terms

The introduction summarizes the purpose of the *TOS*. The rationale provides the theoretical and methodological approaches which serve as a framework for an interpretation of students' communicative proficiency. The third section describes how to use the *TOS*. The glossary of terms defines terminology used in the *TOS* and in the *TOS Usage Manual*.

Phase III: Toward a validation of the TOS

It was recognized that before the *TOS* could be validated and be of practical use to teachers, it was necessary to determine:

— whether the selected *TOS* interactional contexts sample valid presentations of students' classroom interactions;
— whether the three questions for each interactional context solicit from the observer an accurate description of the observed students' functional language abilities;
— whether behaviors described by teachers focus on a description of functional language use;
— whether it is possible to identify students' functional abilities through observation of selected classroom events; and
— whether it is possible to develop a representative number of

communicative performance indicators based on identification of functional language abilities.

In order to clarify these issues and in preparation for field testing of the *TOS*, participants were further trained in the use of micro-ethnographic/sociolinguistic field methods to identify how children use language for functional purposes. The workshop was organized and implemented by Charlene Rivera and Carmen Simich. It was expected that participants would gain a better understanding of what students need to know in order to accomplish communicative tasks during classroom interactions, with the goal of relating this understanding to the observation tasks outlined in the *TOS*. The workshop was organized as follows:

— a review of basic concepts of language proficiency and language proficiency assessment;
— a review of the anthropological orientation of "doing ethnography" in classroom settings;
— a review of the nature and intent of the *TOS*; and
— a formal introduction to functional uses of language in the school, home, and community settings and their relationship to the teacher observation tasks outlined in the *TOS*.

The field testing of the *TOS* was incorporated into the two-day session. Teachers were paired and assigned to different schools to observe students from kindergarten to ninth grade in chosen instructional events. Each teacher recorded his/her observations individually. The half day observations were to be recorded in terms of functional language used by the observed students and other participants, e.g. teacher, peers, etc. Two teachers were assigned to observe the same student in order to compare observations and increase observer reliability. Following the observations, instructors and participants discussed the problems and rewards of the experience. Based on their insights into the process, small groups reviewed the experience, brainstormed, and discussed possible "indicators" of communicative proficiency. Participants also made recommendations for changes in *TOS* content and format.

The next stage consisted in the development of criteria for analyzing the *TOS* field test results. The finalization of this process took place in a two-day meeting in late May, 1981, a meeting between ALPBP project personnel and a representative from TUSD. The criteria agreed upon were:

— whether the observer answered the three questions for each of the four social contexts posed in the *TOS* (see Table 3);

— whether the observer provided a complete and accurate description of the social contexts observed;
— whether the observer described a student's behavior in terms of functional language use; and
— whether the observer's summary of the observation recommendations for student placement were representative of their description of the student's functional language abilities.

Because the *TOS* was at the field test stage, the ALPBP staff were concerned that TUSD would attempt to identify "indicators" of communicative proficiency based only on the limited field test. However, after reviewing the field test results, the concensus of the ALPBP staff and the TUSD representative was that, at most, the data could provide a sample list of communicative functions related to language proficiency identified at the time of the field test. Most importantly, it was concurred that the data could not compensate for further ethnographic/sociolinguistic research into children's "ways of speaking" (Hymes, 1972, 1974) or functional uses of language are available to participants in school settings.

Conclusion

In this concluding section, the limitations and significance of the ALPBP teacher training program in Tucson are described. The purpose is to provide an understanding of the potential benefits in utilizing an ethnographic/sociolinguistic approach to language proficiency assessment.

Limitations of an ethnographic/sociolinguistic approach to language proficiency assessment

The limitations of the approach were found to be related to its implementation in actual classroom situations rather than to its conceptual framework (Philips, this volume). The most significant determinants of successful implementation in Tucson were found to be:

— the working relationship between teachers and administrators;
— the time required to become familiar with the ethnographic/sociolinguistic orientation to language proficiency assessment;
— the educational background of teachers; and
— the characteristics of the ethnographic/sociolinguistic approach.

The working relationship among TUSD educators

Co-operation of educators to participate in any training program is highly related to the working relationship between teachers and administrators. In the case of TUSD, some tension was evidenced between teachers and administrators because of inadequate communication between the two. On the one hand, teachers sometimes felt impotent and frustrated because they were not always sufficiently informed about the administrative details which affected them. On the other hand, it was evident that internal school district changes and pressures were reflected in the administrators' relationship with the teachers, and for this reason, administrative details were not always communicated to teachers. Despite this tension, the gradual involvement and acceptance of the ideas presented during the ALPBP training sessions became a motivating force for both teachers and administrators to co-operate fully.

The time factor

Time to assimilate basic theoretical concepts and to become experienced in their application was found to be a problematic aspect in the training of the Tucson teachers. The time alloted for training was negotiated by ALPBP staff with the TUSD liaisons and was limited primarily by district constraints.

Although each of the three phases of the training program was carefully planned, difficulties arose in co-ordinating sufficient leave time for teachers to attend extended training sessions. Short intermittent sessions were not generally possible because the major consultants were not in the Tucson area. The participating teachers found that the short intense training sessions did not always allow sufficient time to absorb and understand the new theoretical concepts being introduced. One teacher summarized the feeling by indicating that the "time (was) too rushed". She felt "overwhelmed with information". Other teachers suggested that more time should have been given for additional practice and demonstration of observational techniques. Ideally, participants concurred, training sessions should be distributed throughout the school year to allow for clarification of theoretical concepts and their application in the classroom.

Teacher educational background

Teachers do not generally have a background in child language development or second language acquisition issues. They are not familiar with communicative patterns of interaction of multicultural/multilingual student populations; nor are they familiar with the rationale for assessing language proficiency. In Tucson, it was found that teachers highly correlate English language proficiency with knowledge of discrete grammatical/ phonological items. The participant survey (Table 1) confirmed that bilingual educators were not consciously aware of how socio-cultural variables influence the manner in which morphological, phonological and lexical items are integrated into cohesive discourse. Teachers' concerns regarding the assessment of students' language proficiency were, in general, focused on ease of test administration and interpretation of test results, rather than with the nature and scope of children's language and its valid measurement. A general recommendation from the instructors who worked with the teachers was that courses in linguistics, including child language development, second language acquisition, and language proficiency assessment, be integrated into undergraduate programs so that the new generation of teachers is prepared to deal with the complexities of assessing the language proficiency of language minority students.

Characteristics of the ethnographic/sociolinguistic approach

The approach requires systematic observation, by a participant observer, of students' language use in naturally occurring communicative situations in different domains: community, home and school. The role of participant observer has two dimensions: that of a detached, objective observer, and that of an active participant. As such, it requires a person to observe and, at the same time, participate in communicative interactions from a detached yet focused perspective.

In attempting to utilize this approach in the *TOS* it was found that this dual role can, and generally is, problematic because it requires that the teacher attend to the communicative behaviors of one student while simultaneously maintaining the teacher role and provide meaningful learning activities for all students in the classroom. However, because of the nature of the *TOS*, which favors observations by participants who already have an "insider's" knowledge of social rules of language use in each individual classroom, it was decided to use this approach.

Significance of the ethnographic/sociolinguistic approach to training teachers in language proficiency assessment issues

Despite the limitations described above, there were several significant outcomes from the ALPBP teacher training approach to language proficiency assessment. The major outcomes were related to:

— teachers' awareness of the holistic nature of language;
— changes in teachers' philosophy of education, as reflected in their self-assessment of classroom organization and management practices; and
— the development of an ethnographic/sociolinguistic language proficiency instrument, the *TOS*.

Teachers' awareness of the holistic nature of language

The holistic orientation to the nature of language and language proficiency assessment is an important aspect of the ethnographic/sociolinguistic approach to language proficiency assessment. Within this non-traditional approach, language proficiency is defined as knowledge of the grammar of a language together with knowledge of the rules of language use. In addition to linguistic variables, sociocultural and sociolinguistic variables, such as setting, participant(s), topic(s) of interaction, language(s) used at home, school and community are acknowledged. This approach is in contrast to the more traditional one where the major criterion for evaluating language proficiency is knowledge of specific grammatical and phonological items without consideration of the rules of interaction and other sociocultural and sociolinguistic variables that affect communication.

The observations of children's communicative interactions and class discussions provided the opportunity for teachers to become more conscious of the influence of sociolinguistic factors in children's language use. Awareness of the holistic nature of language motivated participants to re-analyze their understanding of language use and its role in classroom communication and learning. One teacher summarized, "I gained additional insight into communication as a whole package". Another teacher said, "I now understand communication is not only verbal". One teacher indicated, "(I am now) more observant of the manner in which children communicate . . . I have learned to focus on the function of communicative behaviors . . . to not only listen to what is or is not said but to pay more attention to *how* the message is communicated".

Changes in philosophy of education

The understanding and acceptance of the ethnographic/sociolinguistic approach and subsequent changes in philosophy of education were evidenced by comments and discussions between participating teachers and instructors. Through the training, teachers became more conscious of the need to expose children to different situations in order to promote motivation and learning through a variety of communicative interactions with different participants in various social contexts. This understanding influenced some teachers to modify their views regarding classroom organization and management. One teacher indicated, "(I now) organize physically in order to allow for more freedom of interaction". Another teacher stated, "I feel an increased sensitivity to the perceptions children have of their environment, especially of their school environment. I feel more acutely aware of the various levels of activity occurring in the classroom and school".

The development of the TOS

The development of a non-traditional instrument, the *TOS*, was another significant outcome of the ALPBP training. The *TOS* is the first instrument which attempts to relate focused teacher observations of students' functional language use in classroom settings and communicative proficiency. The development of the *TOS* is important because it has the potential of providing teachers with an instrument which acknowledges the wide range of communicative abilities of language minority students. Although the *TOS* itself is not yet validated and possibly never will be, it represents an important innovation in language proficiency assessment practice which has far reaching implications for educators servicing language minority students.

APPENDIX A

Section III: Description of Observation data

If you do not understand the student's home language, check this box. ☐

Describe the student's communicative competence in English. Based on your observations, specify the social contexts in which the student is skilled in both languages and those in which the student is skilled mainly in one language.

_____

_____

_____

_____

_____

_____

_____

_____

_____

Teacher Observation System

Section 1: Background information

Student Information:

Name _____ Date _____

Sex _____ Grade _____

Age _____ School _____

Birthdate _____ Teacher _____

Metric _____ Cultural Background _____

Language(s) spoken in the home (choose as may as needed):

English _____ Spanish _____ Other (specify) _____

Language(s) spoken in the neighborhood (choose as many as needed):

English _____ Spanish _____ Other (specify) _____

Has the student ever been in a bilingual program? If so in what grades?

Optional Student Information:

If available, provide the following information:

1. Has the student ever attended school outside the U.S.? Where?

2. What language does the student use to communicate with: Parents _____ Sibling(s) _____ Peers _____

Teacher information:

1. What language(s) do you speak or understand? Check appropriate ones.

	English	Spanish	Other (specify)
Speak			
Understand			

2. Are you implementing a bilingual program?

Yes____ No____

3. Comment regarding teacher knowledge of other languages and nature of educational program being implemented. Describe the language(s) used in the classroom for instructional or social interaction.

_____

_____

_____

_____

_____

_____

_____

_____

_____

_____

_____

Teacher comments (include factors such as physical, emotional, social, etc. that may affect the student's ability to communicate).

_____

_____

_____

_____

Section II: Teacher Observation Data

	Interactions		Interactions	
	(a) ADULT-DIRECTED INSTRUCTIONAL Social Context	(b) PEER GROUP INSTRUCTIONAL Social Context	(a) ADULT-DIRECTED INSTRUCTIONAL Social Context	(b) PEER GROUP INSTRUCTIONAL Social Context
Before starting the observational tasks read the usage manual concentrating on pp. 4–9.	Teacher-assigned/whole group	Self-selected Small group Teacher-assigned Small group	Teacher-assigned/whole group	Self-selected Small group Teacher-assigned Small group
Directions Observe each of the following interactions: (a) Adult-directed instructional; e.g. content area instruction; (b) Peer group instructional, e.g. learning centers, committee work, etc.; (c) Non-instructional, e.g. playground, cafeteria, free choice activities; (d) Other (optional) Describe the interactions observed next to the appropriate questions. Observation Questions	Describe: No. of participants ____ Type of class ____ Language used by students Language of instruction Expected class performance	Describe: No. of participants ____ Type of class ____ Language used by students Language of instruction Expected class performance	Describe: No. of participants ____ Type of class ____ Language used by students Language of instruction Expected class performance	Describe: No. of participants ____ Type of class ____ Language used by students Language of instruction Expected class performance
1. What language(s) and/or nonverbal behavior are used by the student to communicate?				
When the child does not communicate verbally, what evidence do you see that indicates understanding? Describe the behavior observed.				

2. When the student does not seem to understand, what does she/he do to clarify the situation? Describe the communicative behavior observed.

3. Does the student follow the implicit and explicit rules of communication of the social context you are observing?

Notes

1. This paper was prepared as part of the Assessment of Language Proficiency of Bilingual Persons (ALPBP) project. The teacher training component was implemented in cooperation with District I, Tucson, Arizona.
2. Carmen Simich-Dudgeon was the ALPBP Associate. Her major responsibility was to assist in the implementation of the teacher training component of ALPBP project. Charlene Rivera was the ALPBP Project Director, responsible for the implementation of all aspects of the project.

References

Briere, E. 1979, Testing communicative language proficiency. In R. Silverstein (ed.), *Occasional papers on linguistics: Proceedings of the Third International Conference on Frontiers in Language Proficiency Testing.* Carbondale, Illinois: Southern Illinois University.

Chomsky, N. 1965, *Aspects of the theory of syntax.* Cambridge: M.I.T. Press.

Cummins, J. 1980, The exit and entry fallacy in bilingual education. *NABE Journal,* 3, 25–59.

Fillmore, L.W. 1976, *The second time around: Cognitive and social strategies in second language acquisition.* Unpublished doctoral dissertation, Stanford University, Department of Linguistics.

— 1979, Individual differences in second language acquisition. In C. Fillmore, D. Kempler – W. Wand (eds), *Individual differences in language ability and language behavior.* New York: Academic Press.

Genesee, F. 1983, Response to Jim Cummins: Language proficiency and academic achievement among minority students. In C. Rivera (ed.), *Language Proficiency and Academic Achievement.* Clevedon, England: Multilingual Matters Ltd.

Halliday, M.A.K. 1973, *Explorations in the functions of language.* London: Edward Arnold Publications.

Hymes, D. 1964, *Language in culture and society.* New York: Harper & Row.

— 1972, Models of the interaction of language and social life. In J. J. Gumperz & D. Hymes (eds), *Directions in sociolinguistics.* New York: Holt, Rinehart & Winston Inc.

— 1974, *Foundations in sociolinguistics: An ethnographic approach.* Philadelphia: University of Pennsylvania Press.

Tough, J. 1974, Children's use of language. *Educational Review,* 76(3), 166–79.

Tucson Unified School District (TUSD) 1981, *Language proficiency measure (LPM).* Tucson, AZ: TUSD, Testing Services Department of Legal and Research Services Division of Planning Analysis and Management.

Wilkinson, A. 1975, *Language and education.* London: Oxford University Press.

An anthropological linguistic perspective on uses of ethnography in bilingual language proficiency assessment

Muriel Saville-Troike
University of Illinois at Urbana-Champaign •
Champaign, Il

A clear consensus was voiced at the LPA Symposium that whatever is measured by traditional language proficiency tests — pronunciation, grammar, vocabulary — does not adequately reveal the linguistic requirements necessary for success in school. Even if the students being tested prove to be "ideal speakers" and could produce all and only grammatical sentences in English, as Dell Hymes (1966) observed over a decade ago, they would be put in mental institutions if they went around trying to do so. More adequate as a target for language assessment is "communicative competence".

The communicative competence of speakers is a body of knowledge and skills which involves not only the language code that they use, but also what they can say to whom, how they should say it appropriately in any given situation, and even when they should say nothing at all. It involves interaction skills such as knowing how they may develop conversations, and also knowing how to avoid becoming involved in a conversation if they prefer to be engaged in some other activity. It involves receptive as well as productive facility, written as well as oral modes of communication, and non-verbal as well as verbal behaviors. Communicative competence further involves having appropriate sociocultural schemata, or the social and cultural knowledge and expectations that speakers/hearers/readers/writers are presumed to have which enables them to use and interpret communicative forms. The concept of communicative competence must thus be embedded in the notion of cultural competence: interpreting the meaning of linguistic behavior requires knowing the cultural meaning of the context within which it occurs.

The task of determining and testing for the specific linguistic knowledge and skills required by the education process is made even more complex by the fact that "competence" (as language itself) must be considered a variable phenomenon in at least two basic respects. First, since communicative competence refers to knowledge and skills for contextually appropriate use and interpretation of language in a community, it refers to the communicative knowledge and skills shared by the group; but these, by their very nature, must reside variably in its individual members. Problems arise when individual competence is judged in relation to a presumed ideal speech community, or assessed with tests given in a limited subset of situations which do not represent the true range of an individual's verbal ability. The problems are particularly serious when such invalid judgements result in some form of social discrimination against the individuals, such as unequal or inappropriate educational treatment.

Different modes, channels, and functions represent a second kind of variability. The relatively decontextualized nature of written texts may well require a different subset of skills for successful expression and interpretation than does face-to-face communication through an oral medium, for instance. The same may be true for the use of language in some types of cognitive processing. This may account in part for the fact that often individual students may appear to have a very high level of communicative competence, at least in some contexts, and yet not perform well in school. The problem in this case may well be that some researchers are restricting their use of "communicative" to apply only to direct personal interaction, rather than to all uses (and non-uses) of language and other symbolic systems.

A key example of the relativity of "competence" was provided by Shana Poplack (see chapter, this volume) in her report of research on Puerto Rican children in New York. It is clear that they possess communicative competence that is appropriate and sufficient for oral communication within the bilingual community within which they live, yet many of these children are not succeeding in English-medium schools. They do not meet the language expectations of English teachers, nor do they possess the necessary language skills for school-related tasks. If they return to Puerto Rico they neither perform well in Puerto Rican schools, nor meet the language expectations and requirements in Spanish for that context. While these children are competent in language for some communicative purposes, they are not competent in the middle class, formal, public, context-reduced language varieties that are being required for successful achievement in the schools.

One major task before educators is to identify the subset of language-related knowledge and skills which constitutes a core requirement for school achievement at various levels. At the same time, it is important to recognize that gathering data on students' language use in non-school contexts is also relevant to this focus. It is, in fact, essential if educators are to make any valid interpretation of the results from tests given in a limited range of situations in relation to the true range of students' verbal ability. Language use in one situation can only be understood as part of a larger whole. Its psychometric representativeness can be established only on the basis of sampling a large variety of situations. Perhaps, after all, Troike (1983) will prove to be correct in proposing that school achievement reflects the degree of acculturation to the specific Western subculture of the school.

A second issue which was addressed throughout the symposium was that of methods and instruments for assessing communicative competence or language proficiency. As with the inadequacy of traditional language tests to determine students' ability to learn effectively through the medium of English-only instruction, a clear consensus has also been expressed to the effect that no single assessment procedure can ever be trusted to provide information which may be used for important decisions about an individual's appropriate educational placement and treatment. Those who approach this topic from an ethnographic or sociolinguistic perspective consider it crucial that elicitation and assessment of language proficiency include at least some data collected in a natural context. However, any claim to validity and reliability should also show concern for interlocutor and situational effect on linguistic performance.

One exemplary procedure has been reported by Gladys Knott (1981). It begins with naturalistic observation of the classroom as the basis for developing a functional criterion reference measure or "communicative competence profile", in which the students' language is assessed in relation to these criteria in the same context. Another model procedure would result from Richard Duran's (1983) suggestion of developing a "map" of the school day from the perspective of the students, with what they perceive they do at school providing a natural context within which to study the functions of language and to assess communicative competence. Yet another is the kind of microanalysis conducted and reported here by Flora Rodríguez-Brown and Lucia Elías-Olivares (see chapter, this volume), with language proficiency assessment based in part on hours of videotaping each child in school, at home, and in the community setting.

These procedures are, of course, not practical for assessment of all students for placement purposes: children arrive at school and, usually the same day, must be assigned to a program and put in a classroom. Ethnographic methods are very important, however, for providing baseline data on how students use language in various contexts, and on how it relates to their educational achievement. Once baseline criteria are established, naturalistic observation should be included in the assessment of all students, at least for program exit purposes (e.g. for determining whether or not they have the language proficiency to succeed in English-only instruction), and for follow up evaluation (e.g. for determining whether students who have previously been judged "proficient" in English do indeed have the competence to meet instructional requirements without bilingual education or additional native language support).

Assessment through naturalistic observation can most practically and efficiently be conducted by the students' teachers. Training to prepare them to do this is another issue which has received serious consideration during this symposium. This is a very promising direction both for improving teacher assessment and for overall teacher training, but a note of caution must be added here for anyone who might also see this as an "easy" solution. Ethnographic classroom observation requires skill and training, and to ask untrained teachers to summarize their observations will not likely yield valid or reliable data on students' communicative competence. This caution is reinforced by Shana Poplack's (see chapter, this volume) discussion on the discrepancy between reported and observed language use, and also by reports by Steve Chesarek (1981), Jim Cummins (1983), and Betsy Tregar (1983) of teachers' over-estimation of students' language ability.

There is some effort being made to simplify observational assessment procedures so that they could be conducted by untrained individuals, but this is of questionable value. Michael Canale (1983) borrows some timely advice from Albert Einstein that we must seek solutions which are as simple as possible but no simpler. After that there is the danger they will become simplistic. The kind of teacher training described by Susan Philips (see chapter, this volume) is far more demanding of them and of her than if they were being taught to use traditional language testing procedures. Yet even that depth of training may not be sufficient. It is questionable whether sufficient training can be imparted in the course of in-service programs.

The potential benefits of ethnographic training for teachers goes far beyond providing them with tools for language testing, and so is not to be judged merely in terms of practicality and efficiency for that purpose. Even more important are the potential benefits for instruction. This kind of training should increase teachers' sensitivity to communication processes in their classrooms, and heighten awareness of the signals students are giving of understanding or misunderstanding. It should also have an effect on teacher attitudes. As Philips reported, observing communicative interaction in the cafeteria and on the playground changed her trainees' perceptions and attitudes about their students' language ability.

The teacher training discussed in this symposium has been of an in-service nature, but training in ethnographic observation which focuses on communicative interaction and other functions of language in the classroom should be part of undergraduate pre-service preparation for all prospective teachers. Such training would help overcome many of the inaccurate judgments presently being made of students' language proficiency, and should help make teachers more effective and sensitive in communicating with children from different cultural backgrounds.

As always, when one attempts to assess the overall contribution of a volume such as this, it becomes clear that we have much further yet to go than we have come. Some of the presentations have illuminated dark corners, others have lit the entrances to long corridors yet to be explored; a few have shown the limits of unproductive directions. Some exciting new ideas have emerged, and there has been some consensus on where we are and where we might go from here, and an appreciation of the task ahead has been greatly increased. Perhaps most important, we have been stimulated to dedicate our energies anew to seek answers which will help improve educational opportunities for the millions of limited English proficient children.

References

Canale, M. 1983, A Communicative Approach to Language Proficiency Assessment in a Minority Setting. In C. Rivera (ed.), *Communicative Competence Approaches and Language Proficiency Assessment: Research and Application.* Clevedon, England: Multilingual Matters Ltd.

Chesarek, S. 1981, *Problems in assessment and evaluation of child language proficiency in native American bilingual schools.* Paper presented at the Language Proficiency Assessment Symposium, Warrenton, Virginia, March

Cummins, J. 1983, Wanted: A Theoretical Framework for Relating Language Proficiency to Academic Achievement among Bilingual Students. In C. Rivera (ed.), *Language Proficiency and Academic Achievement.* Clevedon, England: Multilingual Matters Ltd.

Duran, R.P. 1983, Some Implications of Communicative Competence Research for Intergenerative Proficiency Testing. In C. Rivera (ed.), *Communicative Competence Approaches and Language Proficiency Assessment: Research and Application.* Clevedon, England: Multilingual Matters Ltd.

Hymes, Dell 1966, on communicative competence. Paper presented at the Research Planning Conference on Language Development among Disadvantaged Children. Yeshiva University.

Knott, G. 1981, *Assessment-Intervention for communication development*. Paper presented at the Language Proficiency Assessment Symposium, Warrenton, Virginia, March.

Tregar, B. 1983, The relationship between native and second language reading comprehension and second language oral ability. In C. Rivera (ed.), *Placement Procedures in Bilingual Education: Educational and Policy Issues*. Clevedon, England: Multilingual Matters Ltd.

Troike, R. 1983, SCALP: Social and Cultural Aspects of Language Proficiency. In C. Rivera (ed.), *Language Proficiency and Academic Achievement*. Clevedon, England: Multilingual Matters Ltd.

Index

138